IN PURSUIT OF GOD

A Love Story

PETER SCHULER

IN PURSUIT OF GOD: A LOVE STORY
by Peter Schuler

2nd Edition.

ISBNs: 978-1-953625-10-6 Trade Paperback | 978-1-953625-11-3 Ebook

Copyright 2021 Peter Schuler

Published by Intelligent Design Press. All rights reserved. No portion of this work may be reproduced in any form, with the limited exception of brief quotations in editorial reviews, without express written permission from the publisher. For permissions, or for bulk orders of church, classroom, or library copies, contact info@intelligentdesign.press.

Photographs by Peter Schuler.

Unless otherwise noted, all scripture quotations are from the Revised Standard Version of the Bible, Copyright © 1946, 1952, 1971 National Council of the Churches of Christ in the United States of America. Used by permission. All rights reserved worldwide.

Intelligent Design Press
An imprint of Kelley Creative
Spokane, Washington, USA

In Pursuit of God
A Love Story

by Peter Schuler

INTELLIGENT DESIGN PRESS

To all the Saints
who love and serve the Lord,
the cloud of witnesses
who have gone before us
and my father
who joined them
in 1979.

Contents

1. A Testimony of Love — 1
2. The Beginning — 4
3. Vision of the New Heaven and Earth — 9
4. Joy in the Mountains — 12
5. Safe in my Father's Arms — 19
6. Worship God with Music — 24
7. Photography — 33
8. The Call to Ministry — 36
9. Valleys of Suffering — 48
10. Jesus is Alive — 62
11. The Holy Spirit — 67
12. At the Feet of Jesus — 73
13. Prayer — 77
14. The Call to Live by Faith — 83
15. Spiritual Warfare — 88
16. Visions — 94
17. Forgiveness — 104
18. Born Again — 109
19. Maturity — 113
20. The Power of the Tongue — 117
21. The Last Day Churches — 121
22. Doers of the Word — 130
23. Unconditional Love — 133

24. The Resurrection	137
25. The Prayers of Repentance	141
26. The Path Set Before Me	150
27. The Final Journey	153

1 | A Testimony of Love

As a child I cried out to God in the midst of oppression and hate and the Lord delivered me from all evil and filled me with His Love. I was raised by a mother who tried to kill me with an axe because I didn't go to Thanksgiving dinner, but God's Love is stronger than the hate and He set me free to walk with Him for the past forty-six years. The Father led me to write this testimony of God's Love for me and my love for Him. I want to proclaim God's Grace and Goodness toward me as I have followed Christ for over forty-six years. The Father has been faithful to me through all the seasons of my life. He delivered me from childhood trauma and I have tasted the Glory of His Presence. He put a passion in my heart to know Him and I continue to seek Him every day. Jesus has led me to many glorious mountaintops and through many valleys of suffering. In the seventies, I walked in the Anointing of the Holy Spirit, and in the 1980s, He called me to lay down my life in the Hope of His Resurrection. The Father fulfilled all His promises to heal me and then called me into full-time ministry. For the past twenty-five years, I have served Him in an inner city ministry to the homeless and those in the jails and prisons. I have been His vessel through which the Father poured out His Love to many lost and hurting people. God has called me to share the Good News of His Kingdom to those without hope, and many have believed His Word.

I love the Lord with all my heart, soul, and strength. I love Him because He first loved me. "In this the love of God was made manifest among us, that God sent his only Son into the world, so that we might live through him. In this is love, not that we loved God but that he loved us and sent his Son to be the expiation for our sins" (1 John 4:9–10). I love all that He is and all that He has done. I love His Ways, His Voice, His Goodness and His Faithfulness. I love His Holiness, Righteousness, Patience and Kindness. My only desire is to spend Eternity in His Presence. I want to draw nearer to Him every day. My passion is to know Him regardless of the cost. I pray, "O, Lord don't let me compromise and become lukewarm. Let this passion always burn inside me to seek You with all my heart. I am not satisfied with this world or the things of the flesh. I only want You. I love You, Lord. Burn away anything that is in me that is not of You. I fall short every day, but I run to You and feel Your loving embrace. I hold onto Your Hand, and You lead me through the storm. I need not fear the darkness around me for You are with me. My heart is overflowing with Your love. Hold me close to Your heart and never let me go. I cling to You with all my strength. I put my hand into Yours, and I walk with You. I am safe because You are with me."

I pray that this book will ignite a passion in every reader to seek the Father with all their hearts! Let us lay down our idols and the distractions of this world and fall in love with Jesus! Let Him be our only desire. If anyone lacks a passion for Christ, let him ask, "For every one who asks receives, and he who seeks finds, and to him who knocks it will be opened" (Luke 11:10). The Word promises that the Lord will give the Holy Spirit to those who ask Him (Luke 11:13). "Draw near to God and he will draw near to you" (James 4:8). This is my favorite verse: **"You will seek me and find me; when you seek me with all your heart… "(Jeremiah 29:13).**

Truly, God is Good!

2 | The Beginning

Salvation

After years of childhood abuse and oppression, I found the joy of a true relationship with Christ in 1975 when I attended a Spirit-filled Charismatic Church in the mid seventies. I spent my childhood in darkness but by the grace of God the Lord revealed Himself to me and I was Born Again and filled with His Holy Spirit" I was inspired to give my life to Christ when I saw the Joy and Power of the Holy Spirit in this Church. The Spirit of God entered into me and made all things new. The Father spoke to me, "Awake O sleeper, and arise from the dead, and Christ shall give you light" (Ephesians 5:14). Jesus told me that I had been asleep in sin, and that He had sent His Spirit into me to raise me from the dead. The Father began to reveal Himself to me through His Word. I tasted the goodness of the Lord

and worshiped Him with all my heart. His Presence now filled what had been a "God-shaped hole" inside me. I finally understood that Christ has Risen and Reigns in the hearts of His believers! I walked in great Joy in the Spirit that no one could take away. I loved everyone. Most of all, I loved Him. I stood in awe of His Anointing and His Glory in the Church.

Baptism of the Holy Spirit

During this time, I was Baptized in the Holy Spirit. A brother from the Church asked if I had been filled with the Spirit like in the second chapter of Acts. I replied that I had never heard of Pentecost, baptism of the Spirit, or speaking in tongues. I was filled with the Holy Spirit and began to speak in tongues as we read the account in

Acts 2. The Power of God came upon me as in the days of the early Church and changed my life. Through the Holy Spirit I received the Power of Christ to lay down my life and then the Power to be raised up with Him (John 10:18). Before that day, I had felt unable to obey Christ, but after my Baptism, I have been filled with the immeasurable Resurrection Power of Christ (Acts 1:8). Thank you, Jesus! Every Good and Perfect Gift comes from the Father! (James 1:17).

Fellowship in the Holy Spirit

For about three and a half years, I walked in His Anointing similar to what had been experienced by the early Church in Acts. I began to know the true joy of fellowship in the Holy Spirit as I attended this Charismatic Church several times a week. The worship in this fellowship was so powerful that we would often sing in the Spirit for ten or fifteen minutes between every song. I saw the Bride of Christ all turned to Him in worship as each member would praise Jesus in their own words. We stood in awe of Jesus, and every day was a blessed gift from God. I saw miracles that resembled those in the early Church. Demons were cast out of people sitting in the pews because of the amazing Power of the Spirit in the Church. Jesus spoke to us through His Spirit, and we loved Him with all our hearts. We sat at His feet as He taught us His Holy Word. I studied His Word at the Church Bible School, and often, the Holy Spirit would speak through the teacher straight into my heart. I was so overcome with conviction and revelation that I was often unable to get up out of my seat for about ten minutes after the classes. Jesus began to put a passion in me to know Him. I was in awe of His Glory and filled with unspeakable Joy. I will always thank the Lord for His incredible Grace to allow me to see His Glory in His Church. Those years were truly a taste of Heaven when we will be united with all believers from every age. For three and a half years, I walked in His Glorious Anointing, but the Lord revealed to me that He would soon lead me into a season of suffering when I would be crucified with Christ so that He could live through me to do the Will of the Father (Galatians 2:20).

The Call of God

During these early years, I was called by the Lord when I was driving to a Wednesday night Church service. Suddenly, I was in the Shekinah Glory of God. I looked up and saw hundreds of Angels in circular ascending balconies stretching up to Heaven. The Lord told me to take off my shoes because I was on Holy Ground. He spoke to me, "Thou art My chosen one"; "Thou shalt bless all the nations"; and "I am God". He also crippled my hands and then healed them several minutes later as a sign that He would soon take away my life and then give it back to me. This season of suffering began several years later in 1981 and lasted for seven years. I cannot describe how awesome it was to be in His Presence. Later in the evening, I came to Church filled with joy, and many commented that I was still glowing with God's Glory. The first song we sang began with the words, "I saw the Lord; He was High and lifted up and His Train filled the Temple" (Isaiah 6:1). Thank you, Father, for Your Grace!

Preparation for Suffering

The Holy Spirit began to teach me about the Cross to prepare me for what I was about to suffer. The Spirit would soon lead me into the wilderness to overcome the power of the flesh, sin, and the enemy (Luke 4:1–12). I was called to ministry, but He first needed to Baptize me with Fire to burn away anything that was not of Him (Luke 3:16). Jesus gave me the Power to lay down my life, and later, He would send His Spirit with the Power to raise me up again (John 10:18).

God revealed to me that He would soon discipline me to give me Victory over the sin nature (Hebrews 12:5–11). I asked Him to remove anything in me that was not of Him so that I might know Him (Philippians 3:7–11). I will always remember those Glorious three and a half years when I walked in the Anointing of the Holy Spirit. God had given me a taste of His Presence that would give me Hope during the dark days to come. Taste and see that the Lord is Good! (Psalm 34:8).

Truly, God is Good!

3 | Vision of the New Heaven and Earth

Switzerland

As a youth, God showed me His Vision of the New Heaven and Earth while on a trip to Switzerland in 1974. I was surrounded by His Glory that was shining out of the mountains, hills, and fields. I was in awe of His Majesty that seemed to fill all my senses. God's Word states that in Heaven, we will no longer need the light of the sun, moon, or lamp because His Glory will be our Light. (Revelation 21:22–23). I was in awe of His Glory as I saw everything glowing with His Presence. The Hope of this Vision carried me through many valleys and trials that would come later in my life. Since the days of this Vision, I have held on to His promise that I would spend Eternity with Him in this Glorious New Earth and Heaven. But according to His promise we wait for a new Heavens and a new earth where

Righteousness dwells (2 Peter 3:13). Like Enoch, I will seek to walk each day with God by faith with the hope that one day, I will see Him face-to-face (Genesis 5:22–24, Hebrews 11:5–6). We cannot even imagine the Glory of the Inheritance that is waiting for us in Heaven. "'What no eye has seen, nor ear heard, nor the heart of man conceived, what God has prepared for those who love Him,' God has revealed to us through the Spirit" (1 Corinthians 2:9–10). During this time, the Holy Spirit began to reveal the indescribable reward that God has prepared for us.

The Lord also showed me a Vision of the Church living in complete harmony with all creation in the new Heaven and earth. We will be at perfect Peace with the Father and with each other. I saw houses that were built and placed upon the land according to the Plan and Will of God. Nothing was out of place because everyone lived in perfect obedience to the Father. I cannot explain now how amazing it was to have every part of my body, soul and spirit alive in His Presence. God was in me, around me, and in all creation. I prayed, "Oh, let me dwell in Thy house Forever singing Thy praise. This is all I ask of Thee. I am a sinner, and I don't deserve such a reward, but in Thy Grace and Mercy, let me be close to You Forever. I ask to be next to Thy very heart. Let me lie on Thy bosom and hold on to You Forever. I have cleaved to You in hope through every storm, and I am still with Thee. Thank You. You are Faithful. You have done it all. I cannot boast. All Glory goes to You."

On this earth, I have set this Hope before me every day while I live by faith awaiting His fulfillment of this Vision. I believe that I have entered the last chapter of my life, and I long for the day when

God will call me up to Himself. When I awake, I will be in His Glorious Presence. Hallelujah!

Truly, God is Good!

4 | Joy in the Mountains

Snow Skiing

    I often think of the joy I experienced in fellowship with the Father during the years that I skied down mountains and carved turns in the velvet snow. My passion was to ski with all my heart and all my strength. I loved the beauty of the white snow and the deep blue skies, and I wanted to ski Forever. I prayed, "Thank you, Lord, for the Grace to ski. In Your Mercy, You have allowed me to experience such joy! I am eternally grateful!" I often felt weightless and free as I floated through the fluffy new fallen snow. Many times, I would reach the bottom of the ski hill with my arms raised in pure joy. Those glorious days are not lost, but they are recorded in His Book Forever. During those precious times, He lifted up from the darkness of this earth and held me in His Arms. I was with Father and safe

Thou dost keep him in perfect peace, whose mind is stayed on Thee, because he trusts in Thee. Isaiah 26:3

from the evil of this present world. I will carry the memory of those days in my heart Forever, and I am grateful for His blessings. I no longer ski on this earth, but I believe that God has prepared a place for me in the next life where I will ski in His Presence Forever. Those wonderful days were truly a gift from God, and I will always be grateful. twenty-five years ago, God called me out of the mountains to do ministry in the inner city. I am content and thankful for all those amazing years skiing in God's Presence. Thank you, Lord!

Cross Country Skiing

During those early years, I often experienced solitude with the Father as I enjoyed cross country skiing in the Sawtooth Mountains of Idaho. I glided across the beautiful snow and through the forests for many miles. I frequently skated with my skis across great frozen lakes in the early spring. The air was cold, and the snow was white and pure. I found peace and joy gliding across the ice and snow with the clear blue skies. I thought of His Eternal nature—endless and Holy. He is pure and unstained by this present darkness. The world doesn't know the Father, but He has chosen to reveal Himself those who believe. I am a sinner, but The Lord sees me in the Righteousness and Holiness of Christ. I am pure and white in His eyes like the snow that I often skied across. By Grace, He accepts me without condemnation, and He is pleased with my heart. I cleave to Christ in faith, and nothing can separate me from His Love. I come before Him in reverence and awe and yet without fear. I am safe in His Arms, and He is always with me.

Fly Fishing

The Father taught me to rest in His Presence as I fly-fished on the Idaho mountain streams. I felt solitude and peace as I walked up and down the rivers in fellowship with the Father. I left behind the stress and worry of this life, and I ran after Him as a son runs after his Father. I wanted to be with Him, to be like Him and to hear His Voice. The evil of this world sought to pull me away from Christ, but by faith, I escaped the darkness of this world to spend time with Jesus. I laid down my burdens and worries at His feet, and He was Faithful to take them from me and restore my soul.

Jesus calls us to come to Him at any time, "Come to me, all who labor and are heavy- laden, and I will give you rest. Take my yoke upon you, and learn from me; for I am gentle and lowly in heart, and you will find rest for your souls. For my yoke is easy, and my burden is light" (Matthew 11:28–30). I need Christ every day, and I cannot live without Him. I am in perfect Peace when my mind is focused on Him, but I fall into depression and despair when I take my eyes off Him (Isaiah 26:3). Every day, I bring to Christ my brokenness and my sorrow, and He restores my soul because He loves me. "In peace I will both lie down and sleep; for thou alone, O Lord, makest me dwell in safety" (Psalm 4:8). I am with my Heavenly Father, and all is well! I am now called to minister in the inner city far from the mountains, but I will always cherish the memory of those beautiful days.

Motorcycle Riding

For many years, I explored the mountain roads and trails in Idaho on my dirt bike. Every spring, I rode to Cooper Basin, and I often raced the antelope that ran beside me in the open fields. The land was young and green, and I was safe because God was with me. I frequently rode my bike to the top of the high mountain passes, and the Father met with me and spoke to me as a friend. I looked out over the land below, and I saw the Father as the Eternal Creator who was and is and will always be. Many times, I rode my motorcycle around the Lost River Range and hiked to the high places. I saw His Glory, and I was content. I loved His creation, His animals, but most of all, I loved Him. I was always safe because I knew that nothing could harm me in His Presence. I would take extra gas on the back of the bike and ride all day alone with the Father. I went up many mountain passes and through fields of flowers with the wind on my face. I beheld God's Beauty, and I was safe in the Father's Hands. I viewed a land untouched by the sinfulness of man. I saw the Father as the Creator of all things. He loved me, and I loved Him!

Mountain Bike Riding

I also rode my mountain bicycle on many trails in Idaho. I explored God's Glorious creation, and I was at peace. I felt as free as the wind as I rode down the paths moving side to side with every turn. The Father gave me strength to go up to His High Places. So many adventures. I loved it all. Truly, it was all good for it came from Him. The Father has given me perfect gifts through Jesus. The Lord gave me the ability to explore His creation, and I sought Him with all my heart. God was always with me, and I was satisfied with His Goodness. Thank you, Lord!

Touring on my Street Bike

I have been blessed to ride my motorcycle through Europe and into Canada. I explored His Glorious creation and camped in His forests. I traveled over many high mountain passes and beside rivers and lakes. I have looked up to the stars and saw the expanse of His universe. How awesome and diverse is His creation! How amazing is His handiwork! In this life, we see Him through a dark mirror, and we are now able to experience only a taste of His Glory. Even a taste of God's Glory is amazing! I will spend Eternity seeking to know more of God and exploring His beautiful creation. I can only fall down and worship Him. I am in awe of all that He is and all that He has done.

Hiking in the Mountains

For many years, I hiked up to the top of mountains to escape the darkness of this world and spend time with the Father. I climbed up to the highest peaks to seek Him, and He often spoke to me with a still small voice (1 Kings 19:9–11). He accepted me, and I felt safe. I wanted to stay up there with Him Forever, just as Peter did on the Mount of Transfiguration (Luke 9:28–36). Many times, I climbed up to the Pioneer Mountains in Idaho and spent the day with the Father, often surrounded by several mountain goats. He made my legs strong and agile so I could tread upon His high places. "God, the Lord, is my strength; He makes my feet like hind's feet, He makes me tread upon my high places" (Habakkuk 3:19).

I climbed God's shining mountains, and I looked down upon the golden valleys. I hiked up high mountain passes in the Sawtooth Mountains and viewed His Majesty. I walked in heavenly places, and I beheld His Glory. I loved Him, and I loved His creation. God gave me the Grace to climb to the highest peaks above the darkness below. I often hiked to high places in the Lost River Range and stood in awe of His beautiful creation. When I was in God's Presence, the wild animals were not afraid of me. I was able to hike with the animals and sometimes touch them. I spent many days in the Father's beautiful creation with deer, elk, antelope, moose, mountain goats, bighorn sheep, bears, mountain lions, and even wolverines. The Father showed me that in the next life, we will live in perfect harmony with all of God's creatures. What a privilege to be invited to see God's Glory and talk with Him on those mountains. I am eternally grateful for everything that He has given me. I am a sinner, but He loved me anyway. He was pleased with my heart, and I found favor in His sight. He allowed me to know Him. What a wonderful gift. Through Christ, I am His son, and He is my Father. I sat with the Father on those peaks, and He talked with me as a friend. "Thus the Lord used to speak to Moses face to face, as a man speaks to his friend" (Exodus 33:11).

The Lamb has made a way for us to come at any time into God's Presence through His Blood. He opened a new and living way to the Father through His Death on the Cross. (Hebrews 10:19–22). We must learn to be still and listen for the Voice of God's Spirit (Psalm 46:10). There are many voices speaking to us in this life that come from the flesh, the world and the enemy. But we need to pray for discernment to recognize the Voice of the Spirit in the midst of all the confusion of this present darkness. His sheep are able to follow the Shepherd because they know Him, and they have learned to hear His Voice (John 10:1–28).

Truly, God is Good!

5 | Safe in my Father's Arms

There is a place in the Father's Arms where I can always go to find Love and acceptance. I often get discouraged because this world is full of cruelty and hate. People judge me by outside appearances, and I frequently feel misunderstood and rejected. Man looks at the outside appearance, but God looks at the heart (1 Samuel 16:7). He created me. He knows everything about me, and yet loves me unconditionally. After experiencing persecution from this world, I sometimes get alone with the Father and ask Him if He is angry with me. He always answers me with Words of Love and tells me that He is pleased with my heart. He is full of Mercy and Forgiveness, Goodness and Love. I love to be still in His Presence and listen. The world is going on the road to destruction at an extremely fast pace. The Father is always Patient and is never too busy to spend time with me. He often tells me to slow down and rest in His Presence.

I have spent my lifetime seeking the Eternal Creator of all things. I am amazed at the Glory of His universe. I love His handiwork. He is the Ancient of Days. "Lord, Thou hast been our dwelling place in all generations. Before the mountains were brought forth, or ever thou hadst formed the earth and the world, from everlasting to everlasting thou art God" (Psalm 90:1–2). I love the mystery of God. He is the High and Lofty One who inhabits Eternity, whose name is Holy. He proclaims, "I dwell in the high and holy place, and also with him who is of a contrite and humble spirit, to revive the spirit of the humble, and to revive the heart of the contrite" (Isaiah 57:15). He is the Father who "alone has immortality and dwells in unapproachable light, whom no man has ever seen or can see" (1 Timothy 6:16). He is High above all things but always comes to us when we cry out for help.

My highest goal is to know Him. "Thus says the Lord: 'Let not the wise man glory in his wisdom, let not the mighty man glory in his might, let not the rich man glory in his riches; but let him who glories glory in this, that he understands and knows me, that I am the Lord who practice kindness, justice, and righteousness in the earth; in these things I delight, says the Lord" (Jeremiah 9:23–24).

There are many counterfeit gods on this earth with many names, but there is only One True God who is the Creator of all things. "For although there may be so-called gods in heaven or on earth-as indeed there are many 'gods' and many 'lords'- yet for us there is one God, the Father, from whom are all things and for whom we exist, and our Lord, Jesus Christ, through whom are all things and through whom we exist" (1 Corinthians 8:5–6). The Word of God makes it clear that the many religions of this world are a result of man's attempt to make a god or gods out of their own understanding, but there is only One True Creator (Acts 17:22–31). I choose not to follow counterfeit religion, but I will seek the One Living God. I am not interested in man's opinions of who God is (religion), but I desire a relationship with my Heavenly Father. The Word promises that everyone who seeks Him with all their hearts will find Him (Jeremiah 29:13).

The Word of God informs us that evidence of God's existence is clearly seen in that which He has created. Many have refused to honor the Father and give thanks to Him, and their minds became darkened (Romans 1:18–32). I bow down before the Father and honor Him and give Him thanks for all that He has done and for all that He is. When I look at a beautiful mountain or a peaceful lake, I immediately see the One who created it all, and I worship Him. I choose not to exchange the Glory of the Invisible God for things made by man. I will Worship the Father Forever!

I love the Father with all my heart. He is the Eternal Creator, the Ancient of Days, the Most High God and the High and Lofty One who inhabits Eternity. He is a Mysterious God who dwells in unapproachable Light, but He is also my Father who Loves me with an Everlasting Love. The Lord proclaims, "I have loved you with an everlasting love; therefore I have continued my faithfulness to you." (Jeremiah 31:3). I am safe in His Arms Forever. I will rest in His Presence for all of Eternity! I pray, "Let me dwell in Your House where no one can steal my joy. I love Your Goodness, and I love Your Beauty. I love Your Glory and Your Presence. I love Your Truth, and I love Your

Faithfulness. I love Your Patience, and I love how You Love me. I love You, Father, with all my heart, all my mind, and all my strength!"

My desire is to walk in continuous fellowship with the Father every day of my life. For many years, I have risen up in the morning, intending to walk all day with Him, but I would frequently fall short. In my weakness, I would allow the flesh, the world, and the enemy to distract me from Christ. I have sometimes felt that my walk with God was a failure because of my difficulty keeping my eyes focused on Him. I read the Gospels, and I saw how Jesus walked perfectly with the Father. Every word, action, healing, and miracle that He accomplished on this earth was according to the perfect Will of God. Jesus stated, "And he who sent me is with me; has not left me alone, for I always do what is pleasing to him" (John 8.29). I asked the Father for help, and He began to reveal to me that Christ in me can walk in fellowship with the Father! What a revelation! God doesn't expect us to do anything on our own. We will never be able to attain righteousness under the Law. The Father gives us Grace to walk with Him through Christ. His Power is made perfect in our weakness (2 Corinthians 12:9). In the New Covenant, Christ in us fulfills the law and walks in perfect obedience to the Father. I am crucified with Christ. I no longer live, but Christ now lives in me doing the perfect works of the Father through me.

God is Light, and we must walk in the Light of the Truth to remain in fellowship with Him (1 John 1:5–9). We walk in the Light when we come to Jesus so that He can expose our sins (John 3:19–21). When we confess our sins, the Father is faithful and just and will forgive our sins and cleanse us from all unrighteousness (1 John 1:9). Anything exposed to the Light becomes Light. (Ephesians 5:13). We are then covered in the Righteous Blood of Christ and walk in the Light as He is in the Light.

I have learned to come to the Father every day. When I fail, I ask for forgiveness and then continue to seek Him. Enoch walked with God for three hundred years in a world of darkness and sin. He had no Church, books, radio, or TV to support him. He walked so close to the Lord that He took him right into Heaven (Genesis 5:22–24). Every day, he drew nearer to God and left behind this world of evil. The Father gradually became everything to Enoch, and he walked right into Eternity. I pray, "O Lord, let me walk with You like Enoch!"

The fruit that is produced when we walk in fellowship with the Father will glorify Him Forever. "But the fruit of the Spirit is love, joy, peace, patience, kindness, goodness, faithfulness, gentleness, self-control; against such there is no law" (Galatians 5:22–23). We produce fruit only when we are connected to Christ for apart from Him we can do nothing (John 15:1–6). In our pride, we try to live our lives in the flesh independently from Him, but these works will be burned up at the Judgment Seat of Christ as wood, hay, and stubble. The works that Jesus does through us according to the Will of God will remain Forever (1 Corinthians 3:10–15).

Truly, God is Good!

6 | Worship God with Music

Worship God in His Creation

    I have worshiped the Most High God on the highest peaks and in the darkest valleys. He gave me the ability to sing and play guitar so I could worship Him Forever. I have sung to the Father from mountain tops, along gentle streams, and beside clear blue lakes. I have praised the Lord while gazing on His Beauty and in awe of His Splendor. From snow-covered peaks to flower-filled meadows, I sang praises to my God with a joyful heart. The Glory of His Presence fell upon me as I lifted my voice to the Heavens. I entered into the gates of His Presence with thanksgiving and praise (Psalm 100:4). I drew near to Him, and He drew near to me (James 4:8). I was filled with the Joy of His Presence, and the Holy Spirit lifted me up into Heavenly places. The Father washed away the burdens of this life as my spirit soared

On the glorious splendor of Thy majesty, and on Thy wondrous works will I meditate. Psalm 145:5

into the Heavens far above the darkness of this world. He touched me with His Hand and all creation seemed to come alive. What a privilege it has been to worship the Father during my years on this earth!

Worship the Father in the Jails and on the Streets

Twenty-five years ago, God called me down to the city to bring the Good News of the Gospel to the homeless and those in the jails and prisons. At first, it was difficult to leave the beautiful mountains, but the Father began to teach me to worship Him by faith in the valleys. The Lord called me to lead others to worship Him on the streets, in nursing homes, and in the jails. Many times, in these years of ministry, the Holy Spirit has lifted me up into God's Presence. I have kneeled before the Father in the jails as the Holy Spirit fell upon me. By faith, I saw the same Glory of God on a dirty street or in a prison cell as I did on a mountain top. Truly, God will come to all who call upon Him. He will hear our cry on the highest mountain or in the deepest valley. The Word promises that "everyone who calls upon the name of the Lord will be saved" (Romans 10:13). During these Worship services, I have seen the miraculous Power of the Holy Spirit fall upon those in jails, nursing homes, and on the streets. I have witnessed the Holy Spirit transform the darkest street or jail cell into God's Holy Ground. All things are possible with the Lord! We worship a truly wonderful God!

Worship Him in Tribulation

I have learned to praise God in the storms of my life. Many times, I have worshiped Him when my heart was heavy with sorrow and pain. When I chose to praise Him in tribulation, the Holy Spirit was faithful to lift me up into Heavenly places. Praise opens the door into God's Presence. The story of Job gives us an amazing example of worship. Job lost his whole family and all his possessions in one day. Instead of becoming bitter and angry, he fell on the ground and worshiped God. He proclaimed, "Naked I came from my mother's womb, and naked shall I return; the Lord gave and the Lord has taken away; blessed be the name of the Lord" (Job 1:20–22). Satan's plan was to tempt him to curse God, but Job chose to worship Him instead. Our natural reaction to suffering is to become angry and bitter, but this causes us to fall into the devil's trap. Instead, by faith, we must choose to worship Him in the storm. Job didn't know why his family had died, but he put his trust in God and began to Praise Him.

Worship can also be expressed through sacrifice. The first time worship is mentioned in the Bible is when Abraham offered his precious son Isaac to God (Genesis 22:1–18). The book of Romans defines spiritual worship as the offering of ourselves as a living sacrifice to God (Romans 12:1).

We can touch the heart of God when we praise Him in the midst of great tribulation. I have prayed during times of suffering, "Lord, help me to always praise You in the storm. Keep the song of praise Forever in my heart. Let not the enemy steal my joy. Please keep my heart young and tender, and don't let it become cold and hard. So much sorrow has come upon me from the hate of this world yet my heart ever yearns for Thee. Lord, please don't allow bitterness or resentment to take root in my heart." Surely, God is Good though this world is not. I have praised Him in the midst of great tribulation, crying out for deliverance with much heaviness of heart. The Father placed me in the cleft of the Rock next to His heart (Exodus 33:18–23). I brought Him my brokenness, and He gave me healing. God heard the voice of my cry, and He did not hide His Face when I was in need. God gave me this gift of music, and I have offered it back to Him. How blessed I am to have a Father like Him!

There is great power in worshiping God during times of affliction. Through the ages, men of faith have called upon the Name of the Lord, and He delivered them (Psalm 107). Paul and Silas praised God in prison, and the power of the Holy Spirit began to shake the building. The chains were broken, and the doors were opened (Acts 16:25–34). Praising God in the midst of suffering breaks the oppression and power of the enemy and sets us free from bitterness and anger. Truly, God will hear our cries for help from the darkest pit. "I will extol thee, O Lord, for thou hast drawn me up, and hast not let my foes rejoice over me. O Lord my God, I cried to thee for help and thou hast healed me" (Psalm 30:1–2).

Worship is a Taste of Heaven

Those special times of intimacy with God are stored in my heart Forever. I cherish every moment that I have spent with Him. The Father has not forgotten them; they are written in His Book, and they are hidden in His heart. Someday, in Heaven, we will lift our voices together in worship to the Creator of all things who loves us. When we gaze upon God's Glorious Face, we will fall down before His Throne. It is clear from God's Word that all those who dwell in Heaven Worship Him day and night. We can have a taste of Heaven now by praising Him by faith in the midst of this world of darkness. The Father has invited us to come to His banqueting table to eat with Him in joy. Lift up our eyes to Him in the darkness and choose to worship Him by faith in the midst of tribulation. In this life, we have looked upon Him through a dark glass, but soon we see Him face-to-face (1 Corinthians 13:12). There is no higher purpose for our lives than to love the Father and worship Him with all our hearts.

The Lord has inspired me to write several songs.

Touch me Lord

Verse 1: In a dry desert place I seek Your Face, touch me Lord, touch me Lord. In a dark and dreary land, I reach out my hand. touch me Lord, touch me Lord. You have been my strong tower; You have been my rock; a mighty fortress, a safe shelter, a refuge in the storm.

Verse 2: Lord, Your mercies are new every morning. Lord, Your Love never ends, never ends. Early in the morning I will rise up and seek Thee; late in the evening will I pray, I will pray. And when my life on this earth is done; when my life is through; Forever I'll be in Your Love, Forever in Love.

I See Jesus

Verse 1: I see into Heaven, an open door; I see the Throne now, I see the Lord. The Holy Spirit's lifting me into His Presence where I'm free, I'm free.

Chorus: I see Jesus High and Lifted up; I see His Glory in me; I see His Bride shining so bright; filled with His Glorious Light.

Verse 2: This is my passion, this is my life; I hear His Call now, I see the Light. Seeking His Presence, walking in love, each day with Jesus, filled with His Love, with His Love. (Chorus)

Your Love Took Me Through

Chorus: Your Love took me through, O Lord; Your Love took me through; when no one else was there for me Your Love took me through.

Verse 1: Through the deepest valleys, across the raging sea, on the highest mountains when I couldn't see; through the darkest nights when tears would fall; I cried out Your Name, Lord You were there, You were there. (Chorus)

Show us the Ancient Paths

Verse 1: Show us the ancient paths that our sins have now covered; show us the way You walked, the narrow path of life. Lord, we confess our sins that we have strayed so far away from You. Redeem us with Your Blood that we may praise Your Name Forever.

Chorus: Praise You Forever, we will praise You Forever; Lord, when we see Your Face we will praise You Forever.

Verse 2: Show us the way of the Cross that we may lay down our lives before You. We leave this world behind and walk the way of Jesus. Let Your Word be a Light to our steps; let our eyes now be opened. Awake us from our sleep and we will praise Your Name Forever. (Chorus)

Verse 3: It's a long way from yesterday, it's a long way to travel. I carry some scars with me of the long and lonely battle. When I thought of giving up You sent Your Love inside me. I never would have made it Lord if You weren't there to guide me, inside me. (Chorus)

With My Whole Heart

Verse 1: With my whole heart, with my whole soul, with my whole strength I will worship You. I will run the race set before me; I will lay down my life at the Cross and I will learn to love only You.

Verse 2: Because with His whole heart, with His whole soul, with His whole strength Jesus died for us. He ran the race set before Him He laid down His life at the Cross and through His death he showed us how to love. So behold the Lamb of God, with the scars on His feet and His Hands and let us go forth serving Him.

Verse 3: So with our whole hearts, with our whole souls, with our whole strength let us die for Him. Let us run the race set before us and lay down our lives at the Cross and learn to love only Him.

Come into His Presence

Come into His Presence with a song in your heart: lifting up your hands to the Lord above. Singing I love You, I love You, I love You Lord, with an everlasting love.

In the Name of Love

Verse 1: Another life is taken, another baby dies; in a world of hatred it all seems right. Another man is dying on the streets alone; without a family, without a home.

Chorus: In the name of Jesus, in the name of God, in the name of heaven, in the name of love. In a Christian nation, in the Church of God, any name you're using, it isn't love.

Verse 2: Another home is broken, another family dies; another child is weeping, asking "Why." Another heart is broken, another lie is told; another finger's pointed, another love grows cold. (Chorus)

Riding on the Morning Sun

Chorus: Riding on the morning sun, flyin' with the wind; I'll climb as high as Heaven and I won't be back again. Spread your wings and fly as high as the sky; the truth will open up to you and you will touch the Son.

Verse 1: I'll only remember the good times that we had; I won't even think of the pain in the past. As I walk down this road alone without you; I'll make myself a new life; a home without you. (Chorus)

Verse 2: Dreams keep me going when my heart feels so low; something to hope for when your love isn't there. It keeps my feet a walkin' when I'm walkin' all alone; I'll make myself a new life with each new morning sun. (Chorus)

Verse 3: Life is for dreaming, a new day will dawn; climb to the mountains or sail on and on. When your life is a prison with four walls all around; make yourself a new life and you'll live on and on. (Chorus)

Born Again

Verse 1: "Behold, behold; I stand at the door; I stand at the door of your heart. If you hear; you hear Me knock at the door, then open the door of your heart."

Chorus: "I will come in; I will come in; and I will sup with you and you with Me."

Verse 2: "Drink; drink, from living waters; drink from the Spirit of God. With Joy, with Joy, everlasting; Joy in the Presence of God." (Chorus)

Truly, God is Good!

7 | Photography

I began to worship God through photography when I traveled to Switzerland in my youth. Throughout my life, God has been pleased to show me the Beauty of His creation, and I wanted to record some of the images so that I might share them with others. Many times, it seemed that God was putting on a show just for me. I felt honored to be blessed with such favor. I took the photographs as a testimony of my amazing experiences alone with God. By Grace, the Father showed me sunsets, snow-covered peaks, fields of flowers, amazing encounters with animals, and beautiful reflections on lakes. I loved to observe how the Father had chosen to create the mountains, valleys, lakes, and streams. I learned about Him by seeing His handiwork—the colors He would choose for the fields of flowers or the creatures He created to walk upon His land. I will always stand in awe of all that the Father has created! I see the Glory of the Father in all that He has made.

The darkness of this present world has covered up the true knowledge of God. The Father's invisible nature is clearly seen in all creation yet many choose not to honor or give thanks to Him. Ever since the creation of the world His invisible nature, namely, His Eternal Power and Deity has been clearly perceived in the things that have been made (Romans 1:20–22). I always see the Creator when I observe His creation. In the same way, we know that a painting hanging on the wall was created by a painter. We may not see the painter currently standing next to the artwork, but common sense tells us that someone painted it. The painting did not paint itself. Creation did not create itself. If there is a creation, then there is a Creator. Sin has blinded our eyes from seeing this simple truth. I seek to regain the knowledge of God that has been lost because of sin. The sin inside of me has obscured my vision of God, and I have often asked Him to remove all that is inside me that is not of Him.

Many times, I sat on the shore of clear lakes and was in awe of the perfect reflection of the mountains in the water. I prayed that God would refine me so that I would be a true reflection of Christ. I still have hundreds of photographs of God's beautiful creation, and I keep them as a reminder of all Goodness that He has shown me. I believe that one day, I will wake up in a new Glorious Land where all the Visions will become an Eternal reality. I have tasted the Goodness of the Lord in this life, and I live in hope of a new age where Christ Reigns in Glory.

Truly, God is Good!

8 | The Call to Ministry

The Father leads us through different seasons in our lives, and sometimes, these changes can be a test of faith. I had walked with Him for many years in the mountains, and I had no plans to ever leave. I loved living up there and spending time with the Father in His Glorious creation. I also knew that I must be obedient to Christ's Call on my life. Like Paul, I wanted to finish the race (2 Timothy 4:6). I longed to please God with my life and be a wise and faithful servant (Matthew 25:21). I have always been amazed that my imperfect life could be pleasing to the Almighty God.

In 1994, God began to call me into ministry to the poor and the homeless, but He first needed to change my heart. Earlier in my life, I had felt no responsibility to help the poor because I thought that the government or the churches were responsible to assist them. During

Peter Schuler

Trust in the LORD for ever, for the LORD GOD is an everlasting rock. Isaiah 26.4

this time, I read Isaiah 58:7, which tells us to share our bread with the hungry and bring the homeless poor into our houses. The Father began to put compassion in my heart for those in need. The Father removed my cold, selfish heart and put into me the heart of Jesus. I started to take the homeless off the street and put them into my 10' x 55' mobile home. At one point, I had a complete family of five sleeping in my home.

During this time, my pastor asked me, "What if God has called you to inner city ministry?" I answered that I didn't think that the Lord would ever take me away from the place that I loved because my life, business, and home was up there in the mountains. I was comfortable and had no plans to ever leave. I did not yet know the Plan of God for my life. The Church was planning a three-day trip to a large city for a Pastor and Leadership Conference. I resisted going with them for several weeks. I had not been to a city in about seventeen years. My plan was to buy a house and live the rest of my life in the mountains, but God's Plan was to Call me to inner city ministry. He showed me that my goals were selfish and asked me how I could justify spending all my money on myself when people were perishing without Christ. He called me to leave the comfort of the mountains and follow Him into an inner city to minister to the homeless.

I had saved up money for seven years when the Lord asked me to give it away to the poor and follow Him. I asked Him why He had waited seven years to tell me, and He answered that I had been too busy to hear His Voice. By the Grace of God, I was able to obey His Call and leave everything behind to follow Christ. Many others through the ages have heard the same Call. Some have obeyed while others have become too involved with this world to follow Him. Peter and the other disciples immediately left everything (Matthew 4:18–19). Some were too busy with their jobs, money, and families to obey Him (Luke 14:15–24). Paul's heart was filled with passion to follow Christ. "But I do not account my life of any value nor as precious to myself, if only I may accomplish my course and this ministry which I received from the Lord Jesus, to testify to the gospel of the grace of God" (Acts 20:24).

I have learned to obey the Call of the Holy Spirit and never look back. I returned once to these same mountains for a vacation, but the Joy of God's Presence was gone. The Spirit had moved on and so must I. The Scriptures warn, "Remember Lot's wife. Whoever seeks to gain his life will lose it, but whoever loses his life for my sake will preserve it." Lot's wife looked back to Sodom and was turned into a pillar of salt (Luke 17:32–33). Moses was once faced with a decision to go into the Promised Land without God's Presence or to stay in the wilderness with God. He decided to stay in the desert with the Father (Exodus 33:12–16). I have also decided to go only where the Father leads me. God's Spirit fills us with Joy when we live in obedience to Him. David writes, "Thou dost show me the path of life; in thy presence, there is fullness of joy, in thy right hand are pleasures for evermore" (Psalm 16:11). God is my home. I will not look back.

Inner City Ministry

I followed Christ down to the city, thinking that I was coming back in three days, but God had other plans. During my visit, I had met a Christian Homeless Ministry, and Jesus called to stay with them in their inner city Discipleship House. I didn't know anyone in the area, but I trusted God to take care of me. I was obedient to the Call of Christ and remained in the city for the past twenty-five years. Jesus had called me minister to the homeless and those in the jails and prisons. God has been faithful and has provided for me all these years. I was given the heart of Jesus to unconditionally love the outcasts of society and treat them as if they were Jesus. (Matthew 25:31–46). Jesus taught me to serve the least of these without judging them. The Lord opened doors for ministry, and I preached the Gospel on the streets, four discipleship programs, nursing homes, and several jails and prisons. I found the joy of being a faithful servant to the Call of Jesus. Many were brought to the Lord and saw the Glory of God. I offered my life as a living sacrifice and God's Love has poured out through me to those in need. Like Peter, I had desired to stay on the mountain with God, but I had been called to the valley where many were lost in sin (Luke 9:28–32).

We have been commissioned by Jesus to go out into all the nations and spread the Gospel of Love. (Matthew 28:18–20). I began to see others through the eyes of Jesus and love them unconditionally. Every person is a precious child of God that can be saved, redeemed, delivered, and set free by the Power of His Love. I will never regret the decision to follow Christ into the inner city ministry. It has been a blessing to watch the Holy Spirit work great miracles in people's lives. The Father has called each one of us to spread His Love to others. We will miss the mighty works that the Lord has planned to do through us when we hold back in fear. I have decided to devote the rest of my life to sowing into people instead of seeking my personal gain. I offered my life to the Father so that He could use me as a vessel through which the Love of Christ can reach to be lost. I pray, "Lord, use my life as a humble vessel through which Your Love can flow to others. My life has meaning only when I am a servant walking in love." I pray to the Father, "Remove all selfishness from my heart and replace it with the heart of Jesus. Lord, Love the world through me. Seek the lost, brokenhearted, and afflicted through me. Let me always see the outcasts of this society through Your eyes of Love."

God began to reveal to me that He had called me to preach and lead worship services. I had to step out by faith and overcome my severe fear of speaking and singing in front of people. The Lord soon opened doors for me to teach a one-hour Bible class at the Discipleship House in the city. I was afraid, and it seemed like there was a large Goliath of fear standing in front of me, telling me that I would fail. I stood up, trusted God, and His Strength was made perfect in my weakness (2 Corinthians 12:9–10). I began to teach several Bible classes a day and lead many worship services a week. All glory goes to Him because I know this ministry came from Him. I simply stepped out by faith and let the Holy Spirit speak and sing through me. I do not seek my own words, but I pray for the Spirit to give me the message. The Scriptures clearly state that we need not worry about what we are to say because it is not us who speaks, but the Holy Spirit is speaking through us (Luke 12:11–12). My words have no power, but His Word brings healing and Life to those who hear. I pray before every service for the Holy Spirit to give me His message for His people.

Jesus calls us to be servants and love others as we love ourselves. He came to serve and not to be served (Matthew 20:28). We are commanded by Jesus to humble ourselves, become a servant, and put the needs of others before our own (Philippians 2:3–11). The Love of God was poured out into me through the Holy Spirit, and Living Waters began to flow out of my heart to those in need on the streets, nursing homes, and prisons (Romans 5:5, John 7:38). I began to enter into the Joy of my Master as I was obedient to His Call.

God's Miracles

God has performed many miracles during the past twenty-five years of ministry. I have chosen to enclose several examples. In the late '90s, The Lord had called me to do several weekly nursing home services. One Sunday, as I was preparing for the service in the Chapel, a lady in a wheelchair told me that a terminal patient down the hall had been unplugged from life support and was expected to die several days ago. She believed that there was a reason that he was still alive.

I went into the room, and the man was lying motionless on the bed. The Holy Spirit told me to lead him in a sinner's prayer even though he couldn't physically respond. I prayed with him and then asked the Lord to take him with Angels to Heaven. His two daughters were in the room, and I asked them if they were believers. They told me that they didn't know Jesus, and I led both of them to Christ. I returned to the Chapel, and the lady in the wheelchair joined us several minutes later and told me that the man had just passed away. She stayed for the service and gave her life to Christ during the altar call. She passed away several weeks later. God's Word promises that He works in all things for good and brings life out of apparent tragic situations. I have seen crippled people in wheelchairs stand up with the Power of the Spirit of God. One man who had not spoken or moved for many years began to sing, talk, and laugh when we sang "Amazing Grace."

The Word of God has tremendous Power to change lives. I remember teaching a message at a Discipleship Program on forgiveness. After the class, one of the students confided to me that he had intended to commit suicide later in the day, but he had changed his mind when the Holy Spirit spoke to his heart through the message on forgiveness. He had already written a suicide note and planned to leave his wife and several children. God spoke to his heart to forgive. I have gone to the deathbed of a friend with AIDS who was in the ICU for spinal meningitis. His blood cell count was very low, and we were told that he was terminal. When I arrived, the Holy Spirit directed me to tell him the story of King Hezekiah's healing, and that God was going to give him another fifteen years of life (Isaiah 38.1–5). The Lord healed him according to His Word and extended his life. I have seen the Spirit so powerful in a room full of inmates that all of them were on their knees before God while we sang "We Are Standing on Holy Ground." God has graciously used me to guide hundreds to the Lord, and I have witnessed many healings. I was only the vessel that God used by His Grace, and I will never take any credit for the years of ministry. To Him be all the Glory!

Evangelism

For many years, Jesus called me as an Evangelist on the streets and in the jails. I have seen the Father do amazing miracles to bring sinners to Christ. The Holy Spirit has used me as a vessel to lead people to Christ in cars, fast-food restaurants, parking lots, city streets, alleys, city parks, jails, and nursing homes. I learned to be sensitive to the leading of the Spirit and not to lean on my own understanding. I will share several examples of how the Holy Spirit works to bring people into the Kingdom. In the late 1990s, I chose to ride my bicycle from the Discipleship House where I resided to a park several miles away. Later in the afternoon, I returned to the discipleship, and I heard the Spirit tell me to ride back to the park. At first, I objected because I had just come from the same park, but I returned in obedience to the Spirit. I arrived at a small pond, and I looked across to a dock several hundred yards away. I saw a teenage boy waving at me across the pond. I concluded that the Spirit wanted me to share the Gospel with him. He told me that both of his parents had recently died, and it was clear that he was seeking answers. I had the privilege of leading him to Christ. There have been many amazing encounters with the homeless on the street outreaches. I once told a homeless man that Jesus loved him, and he began to weep and hug me for about twenty minutes. He responded that no one in his entire life had ever loved him. He accepted Christ, and his heart was filled with God's Eternal Love!

Years ago the Holy Spirit led me to talk to a 72-year-old man who was in jail for the first time in his life. I told him that he could have a personal relationship with Christ by being Born Again by the Spirit. He replied that he had gone to Church all of his life and that no one had told him that he must be Born Again. I shared with him the Words of Jesus that we must be Born Again to enter the Kingdom of God. (John 3:3-8). I led him in the sinner's prayer, and I watched as God's Life came into him and filled him with the Holy Spirit. After over 60 years of religion, the Father took him to jail to hear the True Gospel and be saved. During this time, the Father began to give me His Love for patients in a nursing home. He filled my heart with

His Grief for the elderly that were perishing without Him. The Grief was so overwhelming that it seemed to crush me. I began to realize that He loves us more than we could ever know. He showed me that His Spirit had tried to draw them to Christ during their entire lives, but many had resisted His Love to the very end. One day, I remember wheeling a very thin woman in a wheelchair to our service. She looked up at me and said, "I'm dying." I replied, "You need Jesus." She shouted, "No, no, take me back to my room." In sorrow, I took her back to her room, and she passed away a short time later. The Father loved her so much, but she didn't want Him. Many times, my heart has been broken with God's Love for the lost who are perishing. What more could He do? He sent His Son to die on the Cross for all of us.

    I learned not to judge others by outside appearances. One Sunday afternoon, I was at one of our street outreaches praying for guidance from the Spirit. I was asking the Holy Spirit to lead me to the right person. As I prayed, a drug dealer/pimp pulled up in a Cadillac with two prostitutes in the back. He got out of the car and acted like he didn't want to be at the outreach. The Spirit told me that he was ready to hear the Gospel. I talked to him, and he told me that he wasn't homeless like the other people at the outreach. I said, "But you need Jesus." He replied with tears that He did want to accept Jesus and his Lord and Savior. The Father knew that his heart was ready, despite the way he appeared to me on the outside. Sometimes, the Lord calls us to evangelize when it appears "inconvenient" to us. Years ago, I was busy at work, and I stopped at a store to buy some supplies. I saw a young man outside that store who I had taken off the street to stay at my mobile home several months before. He had stolen from me, and I wasn't interested in talking to him. The Spirit told me to share the Gospel with him. I objected and argued that I was at work and too busy. I soon realized how ridiculous it sounded to be too busy to save a soul for Eternity. I then argued with God that this person had stolen from me. He asked me how much a soul was worth. I realized that my excuses were petty from the viewpoint of Eternity. I shared the Gospel with him, and by the Grace of God, he accepted Christ.

I have seen hundreds of souls come into the Kingdom. They were considered outcasts of society—drunks, bums, addicts, drug dealers, pimps, gang members, hardened criminals, and chronically homeless. Society considered them worthless and useless, but in God's eyes, they were His beloved children who had come home to Him. All Heaven rejoiced as these lost souls, who were often rejected and hated by this world, entered into God's Kingdom. The Lord commanded His servants, "Go out quickly to the streets and lanes of the city, and bring in the poor and maimed and blind and lame… that my house may be filled" (Luke 14:21–23. See 14:15–24). The Lord is calling the weak, the outcasts, and the hated in this world to come to Him and live Forever in His Kingdom. "God chose what is foolish in the world to shame the wise, God chose what is weak in the world to shame the strong, God chose what is low and despised in the world" (1 Corinthians 1:26–29). What an honor it has been to love these precious people. Jesus will reward all those who love, serve, and give to those in need (Matthew 25:31, 46).

Have we been obedient to the Great Commission of Jesus to "go therefore and make disciples of all nations, baptizing them in the name of the Father and of the Son and of the Holy Spirit, teaching them to observe all that I have commanded you, and lo, I am with you always to the close of the age"? (Matthew 28:19–20). The Church is called to be ambassadors for Christ, God working through the us with the ministry of reconciliation to a lost world. "So we are ambassadors for Christ, God making his appeal through us. (2 Corinthians 5:17-20). It is Glorious to be used by God to love others as a humble servant. I pray, "Lord, give Your Love for the lost of this world and send me out to a world that is perishing. Help me to love them unconditionally, without judgment or condemnation. Let me be Your ambassador to spread Your message of the Good News of the Gospel. I am not on this earth for my selfish pleasure and enjoyment. I am alive to fulfill Your Call upon my life and do the work of the ministry. Lord, here I am, send me (Isaiah 6:8). I am available to do Thy Will. Let me love those who are rejected and hated by this world."

Truly, God is Good!

9 | Valleys of Suffering

Seasons of Suffering

My favorite time of year in the mountains is the fall, and I love the beauty of the golden leaves. I have spent countless hours looking at the fall colors as the sunlight shined through the trees. The yellow, orange, and red leaves were beautiful against the clear blue skies. I wanted the show to never end, but the autumn winds would blow the leaves off the trees and onto the streams and meadows. I would often think about the splendor of these leaves as they died in the fall. The Lord began to teach me about the beauty of suffering and death. The Father revealed to me that He has called us to walk with Him through times of pain and affliction and also seasons of healing and resurrection. The Lord has made everything beautiful in its time (Ecclesiastes 3:11). He has called us to glorify Him in all things. The

Father had prepared me for this time of suffering by first giving a taste of His Presence in the mid-seventies. The Vision of His Glory gave me Hope as I went through the valley of affliction. I was able to put my suffering in the perspective of Eternity. The Word teaches, "For this slight momentary affliction is preparing for us an eternal weight of glory beyond all comparison" (2 Corinthians. 4:17). Jesus is our example, "who for the joy set before him endured the cross, despising the shame, and is seated at the right hand of the throne of God" (Hebrews 12:2). I kept the Joy set before me as I entered the valley of the shadow of death. I did not fear evil because I knew that God was with me (Psalm 23:4).

The Beauty of the Cross

The Lord began to show me that Christ's death on the Cross was beautiful because it revealed to us the depth of God's Love for us. The Cross demonstrated the passion of the Bridegroom for His Bride who was lost in sin. Christ's death united Him with His Bride and brought deliverance to her from the power of death, sickness, pain, sin, and sorrow. As believers, we are called to take up our crosses and glorify the Father through our surrender to Him (John 21:18–19). The highest expression of our love for the Lord is to sacrifice our lives to Him (John 15:13).

Called to Suffer

The Father revealed to me in my youth that I had been called to suffer on the narrow path that leads to life. The Bible teaches, "For to this you have been called, because Christ also suffered for you, leaving you an example, that you should follow in His steps" (1 Peter 2:21). Jesus has carried me through the darkest times when I lacked the

strength to make it on my own. I wrote a song about this experience: "Your Love took me through O Lord, Your Love took me through. When no one else was there for me, Your Love took me through. Through the deepest valleys, across the raging seas, on the highest mountains when I couldn't see. Through the darkest nights when tears would fall. I cried out to You. Lord, You were there, You were there." The Father began to teach me that His most powerful work was on the Cross. Our natural mind is unable to understand that God's Power to save us comes through the Cross. "For the word of the cross is folly to those who are perishing, but to us who are being saved it is the power of God" (1 Corinthians 1:18). God does the most dramatic work in our lives during the times of greatest suffering. Jesus took me in His Arms and carried me for seven years when my body was full of pain and sickness. By faith, I was lifted up into Heavenly places where God revealed Himself to me in a special way. God preserved my life when my enemies sought to kill me. When I had no strength to continue, I cleaved onto Him when all others had forsaken me. When the season of suffering was over, He spoke His Word of Life and Healing into me. Suffering cannot separate us from His Love. (Romans 8:35–37). God restored my life so that I could fulfill the work to which I had been called. All Glory goes to the Son who is the Author and the Finisher of our faith. He walked the Path before us, and He will carry us to the finish line: Heaven (Hebrews 12:1–2). Jesus taught me to use my eyes of faith in the valleys to see that His Light shines brightest in the darkest times. He walked the Path of suffering before me when He endured the Cross, and He called me to follow Him.

Hip Injury

Jesus had led me through many difficult trials, and He has always given me the Power to lay down my life and the Power to be raised up again (John 10:18). In the mid-nineties, He took me through a time of affliction when I was nearly crippled. The surgeon told me after a six-and-half-hour surgery that there was a good chance that I would never walk again. I had no health insurance to pay for the large medical bills. In addition, my "friend" who was supposedly helping me during this time, relapsed on drugs, stole my debit card and all my emergency money. I was confined to my bed for about two months, and I began to pray five to seven hours a day to my Heavenly Father. Surely, He hears the cry of His Saints. Gradually, the pain lessened, and I was strong enough to read the Word. I started reading at the beginning of Genesis and ended at the last chapter of Revelation.

He lifted me up into Heavenly places, and I spent the next several months in the Spirit with the Lord. It was an amazing time of revelation in the knowledge of Him. I turned over my medical and financial problems to the Father and sought Him with all my heart. God was Faithful to heal me completely, and He miraculously took care of my medical bills and the financial problems. The Father asked me to give Him my burdens and seek Him with all my heart. Like Peter, I learned to walk by faith above the water of my circumstances. We serve an amazing and loving Heavenly Father who is Faithful to deliver us in time of need!

The Seven-Year Illness

God called me to my deepest valley when I was twenty-seven years old. Three years earlier, the Father had spoken a word of Proph-

Though the fig tree does not blossom, nor the fruit be on the vines, the produce ot the olive fail and the fields yield no food, the flock be cut off from the fold and there be no herd in the stalls, yet will I rejoice in the LORD, I will joy in the God of my salvation. Habakkuk 3.17,18

ecy to me that He would take away my life and then give it back again. The Lord showed me a sign by crippling my hands and then healing them. His promise of healing gave me Hope through my seven-year illness. In 1981, I came home from work, and my leg began to swell out to about twice its size. I went to the doctor, and he told me that I could go to the hospital, but it probably would be a waste of money because there was a good chance that I would be dead by the next day. (I went back to see the doctor seven years later to tell him that I had survived, but I was informed that he had passed away.) The swelling spread to my other leg and then to my whole body. My liver and kidneys stopped functioning properly, and I was filled with yellow jaundice. My body was swollen with fluid, and my weight went from about 175 to about 500 pounds. The poisons filled my body and stopped most body functions. The food could no longer break down in my stomach, and it would rot in my digestive tract and then pass through me undigested.

My stomach was so swollen that I was often afraid that it would burst. I would chew the same piece of meat in my mouth for hours because I lacked enzymes in my body to break it down. I developed severe insomnia, and I was able to sleep only a couple hours a week for the next seven years. I lived at night, and I never came outside during the day. The pain in my body was nearly unbearable, and I had the strength to face only one second at a time. I was too weak to even think that the suffering would continue in the future. Jesus gave me the Grace to endure the suffering. He bore the pain for me, and He carried me through these darkest times. All Glory goes to Him!

My body stopped functioning, but my spirit soared with God. The Word teaches, "So we do not lose heart. Though our outer nature is wasting away, our inner nature is being renewed every day" (2 Corinthians 4:16). The Scriptures teach us to live by faith "because we look not to the things that are seen but to the things that are unseen; for the things that are seen are transient, but the things that are unseen are eternal" (2 Corinthians 4:18). My body was wasting away, but my inner nature was being renewed by the Lord. During this time, the Father revealed Himself to me in an amazing way. He also opened my eyes to see the spiritual realm that is usually hidden behind a veil. My body was nearly dead, but my spirit was alive with God. Like John, I was called through the door into the spiritual world that is usually hidden from our eyes (Revelation 4). The Lord allowed me to see the great spiritual battle that is going on around us in these end times. The illness took away my body, mind, and mental health, but my spiritual awareness was greatly intensified. I was dead in the flesh and alive in the Spirit.

As I walked in the Spirit, my body continued to waste away from the results of the sickness. I went through my savings account and lived in total poverty. I wore old clothes that I found in a dumpster behind a local thrift store. By God's Grace, I lived many years with little money and no government assistance. God was always there faithfully carrying me through the darkest times. Sometimes, I went a week at a time without eating. The fluid made me look overweight, but in fact, I was starving to death. I wandered the streets at five hundred pounds filled with poison. People would walk to the other side of the street to avoid me. Others would mock and laugh at my size, appearance, and smell. No one ever stopped to help me. I felt like more of an animal than a human. One day, I stood starving for food outside a grocery store with eleven cents in my pocket watching people buy fifty pounds bags of dog food. At that point, I wished that I was a dog so that someone would have compassion on me and give me some food. Note: for the past twenty-two years, I have been called to work with the homeless and inmates in jails. I now understood what it feels like to be treated as less than human. I seek to treat them with dignity and respect because they are all loved by God. We are all called to serve the least of these as if they were Jesus (Matthew 25:31–46).

At twenty-seven years old, the illness caused my hair to turn gray and fall out. I felt like every molecule of my body had been destroyed. I was so weak that I was unable to read even one line in a book. Gradually, I lost my ability to read and write. I was able to walk only a couple steps at a time. Somehow, in this condition, I had to find money to live. By God's Grace, I survived without any human assistance. I lived at night when the temperatures outside were down to twenty below zero in the winter. Jesus carried me through this illness for seven years. My liver and kidneys stopped functioning, and my immune system was very weak. The poisons that filled my body began to destroy my brain cells. After several years, I began to lose all memory of my past. I had two college degrees, but I no longer knew that $2 + 2 = 4$. I had spent twenty-seven years learning many things that were now lost in a few months. I was once a top athlete, but the illness made it difficult to walk even a couple steps. My appearance was so changed that I became unrecognizable. My "friends" deserted me and offered no assistance. The poisons were coming out of me in the form of sweat, and I smelled like rotten flesh. People would avoid me because of my appearance, size, clothes, and the odor of my body. In this world, I felt like a dead man walking, but by the Grace of God, I still walked with Him in the Spirit. My eyes were yellow from the jaundice, and I was extremely malnourished. My legs were in constant pain and frequently cramped up. I had several heart attacks from malnutrition and lack of potassium. My memory was erased, and I had forgotten who I was and what I had done in my past. I lived one day at a time in survival mode for seven years.

The chemicals in my body also caused me to become seriously mentally ill. I was severely depressed, and I felt that I had fallen into a deep pit. I was very angry and paranoid so I viewed this world as an evil system designed to starve me to death. I developed OCD and lived by many rituals and routines. I was alone and abandoned, but I still had my faith in God and His promise to heal me. I had no medical insurance, no doctors, no friends or family support, but God was with me. I cleaved to Him. I could not save myself, only God could deliver me. Surely, the Lord is near to all those who call upon Him!

Spiritual Warfare in the Valleys

Like Job, I was under intense spiritual attack from the enemy. He hated me and sought to kill me because I belonged to God. I put my life in God's Hands and believed that God would be faithful to carry me through this valley and heal me. In the story of Job, the enemy was permitted to take away Job's family, possessions, and health. But during this time of affliction, God remained in control, and He gave the devil strict boundaries to protect Job. Job didn't understand why all this evil was happening to him, but he put his trust in God. Like Job, I had been called to suffer and be refined in the fire of affliction. I believed that He would rescue me from the power of the evil one and send His promised healing. In the end, like Job, my life was restored, and I was given great blessings. Thank you, Lord!

God Heals My Body and Mind

At the Father's appointed time, He sent His Spirit into my seemingly lifeless body. I stood up on my feet. The Spirit breathed Life into my "dead body," and I was raised from the grave (Ezekiel 37:11–13). He miraculously sent some money to me in the mail to provide for my needs. The promised time of healing and resurrection had finally come! For the next several years, the Father caused the fluids to be expelled from my body at a rate of about seventy pounds a year. Gradually, He taught me how to walk again, and I began to practice every day to regain my strength. I remember the day that I made it up a small hundred-foot hill. I was so excited; it seemed like I had climbed Mount Everest. For several years, the Father took me back through my childhood to restore to me the memory of my previous life. My Heavenly Father who had created me still remembered who I was. (See Psalm 139). Gradually, He healed my body, mind, and soul until I was a new creation in Christ. The Father restored my personality, and He taught me how to do all the sports and activities that I had previously done in my youth. I started to ski, hike, cross country ski, motorcycle ride, and bike ride again. At the beginning of this process of healing, my body was still weak and filled with fluids. Gradually, the Father gave me back my life in the mountains, and I walked with Him again in His Glorious creation. Truly, the Lord is a God of miracles and healing. The Father restored to me what I had learned in twenty years of school. I began to study some GED books, and He helped me to relearn how to read, write, and do basic math. Father chose not to restore my complete memory, but He gave me back what He wanted me to remember. Gradually, I began to talk, think, and learn again. The Lord was my doctor, physical therapist, and my psychiatrist. The Father breathed Life into me and raised me from the dead. I had been crucified with Christ, but now He lived in me Forever! We serve a truly amazing God!

The Father Heals my Heart

The psychological healing took several years. I had developed many serious mental problems during the illness—severe depression, paranoia, schizophrenia, anger, and bitterness. I felt rejected and alone as I lay in my room of suffering. I also developed severe PTSD from the trauma of my illness. God revealed to me that He wanted to heal the hurt and anger that was in my heart. He said that I had roots of bitterness growing inside me from all the cruelty and suffering that I have experienced. The Father began to expose what was in my heart by revealing the causes of my anger. When some current event triggered my anger, God would then reveal to me the causes of the bitterness that had been hidden from my view. He then gave me the choice to forgive and be set free, or hold on to the resentment and be miserable. The healing of my heart took years because the roots of bitterness had accumulated for most of my life. God's Light exposed the darkness, and I chose to let go and be healed (Ephesians 5:8–13). He restored my life and then called me to minister to broken and hurting people. The Father showed me that I would be able to comfort people that were suffering with the comfort that God had comforted me during my illness (2 Corinthians 1:3–6). Looking back, I can see God's Plan and purpose in these years of suffering.

The Cross is God's Plan

The Cross is the center of God's Plan to restore all things unto Him. I prayed to know Him, and He showed me that my flesh (sinful nature) was hindering me from seeing Him clearly. I asked Him to crucify the flesh and remove anything in me that was not of Him. I wanted to go through the fire to be refined so that Christ would be manifested in me (2 Corinthians 4:7–11). God disciplines the sons He loves (Hebrews 12:5–11). This verse became a reality for me–"I am crucified with Christ; it is no longer I who live, but Christ who lives in me; and the life I now live in the flesh I live by faith in the Son of God, who loves me and gave himself for me" (Galatians 2:20). In my previous life, I had lived to do my own will in the flesh, but now Christ lived in me to do God's Will in the Spirit. The old man has died, and Christ now lives! Hallelujah! Great is the mystery of God's ways! I stand in awe of Christ who accomplished all things on the Cross! Christ now lives in us in obedience to the Father. I couldn't obey Him in the flesh, but now Christ in me does what is pleasing to the Father. I pray that every day, there will be less of me and more of Him in my life. I want Him to live through me, speak through me, and walk with the Father through me. Through Christ, we can now have Victory over the flesh and sin! I still fall far short of His Glory every day, but I am amazed that Christ is able to work through me for His Glory!

Truly, God is Good

10 | Jesus is Alive

Jesus is God, and His Glory is far greater than we can now realize. He died, but He is now Alive Forevermore! In my youth, I went to several "dead churches," but I did not yet know the True Risen Lord until I attended a Charismatic Church in the mid-seventies. I became a witness of the Resurrection Power of Christ living in these Saints. I bowed down to Him and shouted, "He is Lord! Jesus is Alive and Living in me!" I joined these believers in worshiping Him when I saw the Glory of the Risen Lord. I asked Jesus to come into my heart, and He made all things new. I prayed, "Thank you, Jesus, for loving me before I even knew You. You gave Your Life for me so I could have a way to be with the Father Forever. You have made all things possible! I will praise You throughout Eternity. All Glory, Honor, and Praise goes to the Lamb that was slain. I can only bow down before You and worship You with all my heart. Jesus is worthy to be Praised!" "Worthy is the Lamb who was slain, to receive power and wealth and wisdom and might and honor and glory and blessing!" (Revelation 5:12).

Jesus is the Revelation of God to man. He is the image of the invisible God. The Father dwells in unapproachable Light, and we know Him because He chose to reveal Himself through Jesus. I love Jesus because He made a way for me to know the Father. "He is the image of the invisible God, the first born of all creation; for in Him all things were created, in heaven and on earth, visible and invisible, whether thrones or dominions, or principalities or authorities- all things were created through him and for him. he is before all things, and in him all things hold together" (Colossians 1: 15–17). Jesus is God. He told Philip, "He who has seen me has seen the Father" (John 14.9). He taught His disciples, "I and the Father are one" (John 10:30). Jesus proclaimed, "All authority in heaven and on earth has been given to me" (Matthew 28:18). Jesus has complete authority over creation because all things were made by Him and for Him. He calmed the storm with His Word (Mark 4:37–41). Jesus has all authority over the enemy, and He cast out an army of demons by His Word (Mark 5:1–20). Later in the same chapter, He showed His Power to heal an "incurable disease." A woman reached out by faith and touched His garment, and the healing Power of Jesus was released into her body (Mark 5:24–34). Mark then records the Power of Jesus to raise a twelve-year-old girl from the dead (Mark 6:35–43). Jesus has absolute authority over creation; the devil, sickness and death. Yet in Mark 6, we are shown that unbelief stops His work in our lives. He returned to His hometown and "could do no mighty work there, except that he laid his hands upon a few sick people and healed them. He marveled because of their unbelief" (Mark 6:1–6). The people of Nazareth knew Jesus in His earlier life and refused to believe that He was God. When Jesus comes into our lives, can He do a mighty work in us?

Who is Jesus? He is the Lamb who died for our sins, but He is also the Lion who will Reign Forever as King. On this earth, he walked as a humble servant and most of His Glory was hidden (Philippians 2:5–11). Years later, John saw Him in His Glory, and he was so overcome that he fell down on the ground as if he was dead (Revelation 1:12–19). The Lord's hair was white as wool, His eyes were like flames of fire, and His Face looked like the sun shining at full strength. John wrote, "When I saw him, I fell at his feet as though dead. But he laid his right hand upon me, saying. 'Fear not, I am the first and the last, and the living one; I died and behold I am alive for evermore, and I have the keys of Death and Hades'" (Revelation 1:17–18).

Jesus is calling us to come to Him as the Savior of the world who takes away our sins (John 1.29). We are all sinners for "all have sinned and fallen short of the glory of God" (Romans 3:23). Through His Church, He is reaching out to the broken hearted and afflicted and calling them to come to Him to receive Mercy. He is not wishing that any would perish and has given all men time to repent (2 Peter 3:9). Some have chosen to come to Him and receive Forgiveness and Eternal Life, while others have refused to bow the knee. We must not delay, for if we refuse His Mercy now we will kneel before Him in Judgment. His return will be a day of rejoicing for His Bride but a day of terror for the world. Those who refuse to ask for Mercy from the Lamb will soon know the Wrath of the Lion who comes to judge the world. "Behold, he is coming with the clouds, and every eye will see him, everyone who pierced him; and all the tribes of the earth will wail on account of him. Even so. Amen." (Revelation 1:7). The world crucified the Lamb when He came two thousand years ago, but they will soon meet the Lion! He will return as the Great and Glorious King, and they will experience His Eternal Wrath.

He opened the sixth seal, I looked, and behold, there was a great earthquake; and the sun became black as sackcloth, the full moon became like blood and the stars of the sky fell to the earth as the fig tree sheds its winter fruit when shaken by a gale; the sky vanished like a scroll that is rolled up, and every mountain and island was removed from its place. Then the kings of the earth and the great men and the generals and the rich and the strong, and every one, slave and free, hid in the caves and among the rocks of the mountains, calling to the mountains and rocks, 'Fall on us and hide us from the face of him who is seated on the throne, and from the wrath of the Lamb; for the great day of their wrath has came, and who can stand before it.'" (Revelation 6:12–17)

Unbelievers have constructed a godless society to shield them from the reality of God and the Lamb. Soon, it will all disappear, and everyone will have to bow before Jesus and acknowledge that He is Lord. Jesus will then sit upon His Great White Throne and Judge all those whose names are not written in His Book of Life (Revelation 2:11–15). Come to Him now before it is too late and receive His Mercy and the gift of Eternal Life. "Thank you Jesus that my name is in Your Book. I need not fear Your return. It will be a glorious day of rejoicing for Your Church. I am eternally grateful for the price that

You paid for my sins so that I may spend Eternity in Your Presence. I will worship You Forever! You are worthy to be praised. You died and are alive Forevermore!"

Truly, God is Good!

11
The Holy Spirit

The Holy Spirit is my life. The Spirit makes all things Glorious, and I am completely dependent on Him for my very existence. My thoughts, words, and actions are dead without Him. I rely on the Spirit to empower me, direct my steps, to give me understanding of His Word, and to reveal the Father to me. He convicts me of sin and guides me to all Truth (John 16:7–11). The Spirit brings Glory and Life to all things. "It is the Spirit that gives life, the flesh is of no avail" (John 6:63). I need Him every second of every day. I seek to be led by the Spirit, walk by the Spirit, pray by the Spirit, and live by the Spirit. The Holy Spirit is God, and He empowers the Church to spread the Good News of the Gospel to all the earth. The Church Age began about two thousand years ago with the Great Outpouring of the Holy Spirit in Acts 2. The Book of Acts

describes how the Holy Spirit Anointed the early Church to evangelize throughout the known world. Jesus proclaims to the disciples, "But you shall receive power when the Holy Spirit has come upon you; and you shall be my witnesses in Jerusalem and in all Judea and Samaria and to the end of the earth" (Acts 1:8). Jesus told His disciples to wait in Jerusalem until they were "clothed with power from on high" (Luke 24:48). The same Holy Spirit is Anointing the Church today to be His witnesses throughout the world.

There is a story which illustrates the Power of the Holy Spirit. A man once bought a chainsaw from a store and brought it home to cut a log. He labored all night and couldn't cut the wood. He brought it back to the store owner who told him that the chainsaw was very effective at cutting wood and that he should try again. The man struggled unsuccessfully for hours that night and then brought it back in the morning. The store owner told him that he would demonstrate how well the saw worked by cutting a log in the back lot. The owner started the saw and the man exclaimed, "What's that sound?" The man had struggled for many hours to cut the log with the chainsaw turned off. In the same way many Christians struggle to follow Christ in their own strength, without the Power and Anointing of the Holy Spirit. We read in Acts how the Baptism of the Holy Spirit empowered the weak Apostles with the Resurrection Power of the Holy Spirit to spread the Gospel throughout the world. The same Power of the Holy Spirit that raised Christ from the grave is in us who believe. (Ephesians 1:17-23.

Twenty-five years ago, the Lord called me to ministry and Anointed me with the Holy Spirit to preach His Word. The Lord spoke these words to me: "The Spirit of the Lord is upon me, because He has anointed me to preach good news to the poor. He has sent me to proclaim release to the captives, recovery of sight to the blind, to set at liberty those who are oppressed and to proclaim the acceptable year of the Lord" (Luke 4:18–19). The Father promised me that the power of His Anointing in me was stronger than any spirit or man that would seek to come against me. The Word proclaims: "Little children, you are of God, and have overcome them, for he who is in you is greater than he who is in the world" (1 John 4:4). I have relied on the Holy Spirit for every sermon and every service for twenty-five years of ministry. I am powerless to preach, sing, or write anything on my own. The Holy Spirit Anointed me to write this book, and my prayer is that this book contains His Words, not mine. I am completely dependent upon the Anointing and Guidance of the Holy Spirit. Thank you, Spirit of Grace! The Lord began to open doors for ministry, and I stepped out in faith to obey Him. Like Moses, I first had to overcome my lifelong fear of speaking: Moses proclaimed, "I am not eloquent, either heretofore or since thou hast spoken to thy servant, but I am slow of speech and of tongue" (Exodus 4.10). I learned to take my eyes off of myself and onto Him. The Father began to ask me to trust Him and let the Holy Spirit give me the words to speak. I now pray, seek the Lord, and let the Holy Spirit give me every message. In the past twenty-five years, the Lord has opened up many doors for ministry in discipleship programs, street outreaches, nursing homes, jails, and prisons. The Word teaches that "it is not you who speak, but the Spirit of your Father speaking through you" (Matthew 10:20). Again the Scriptures explain, "For the Holy Spirit will teach you in that very hour what you ought to say" (Luke 12:12).

All Glory goes to the Father! I cannot take credit for one word, one miracle, or one salvation. It has all been by His Spirit. The Word reminds us, "Not by might, not by power, but by my Spirit says the Lord of hosts" (Zechariah 4:6). The Father has warned me not to use my own intellect, knowledge, or to ever seek my own glory. Paul writes, "When I come to you, brethren, I did not come proclaiming to you the testimony of God in lofty words of wisdom. For I decided to know nothing among you except Jesus Christ and him crucified. And I was with you in weakness and in much fear and trembling; and my speech and my message were not in plausible words of wisdom, but in demonstration of the Spirit and power, that your faith might not rest in the wisdom of men but in the power of God" (1 Corinthians 2:1–5). The Lord has often reminded me of my complete dependence on the Holy Spirit. One night, at a jail service, I was preaching on the Anointing of the Holy Spirit to resurrect the dry bones in Ezekiel 37. The first service was filled with the Spirit, but the next service seemed dead, and my words had no life. I prayed before the third service, and the Father showed me that He was teaching me that my words have no power without His Spirit. I asked for the Holy Spirit to come and the next service was full of Joy in the Spirit. Thank you, Father, for Your Anointing!

I have sought to stay filled with the Spirit throughout the past forty-six years, but I have often failed. I was Baptized in the Holy Spirit in the seventies, but I soon learned that I must continue to seek Him every day to stay filled with the Spirit. The Word promises that the Heavenly Father gives the Holy Spirit to those who keep asking, seeking, and knocking for Him (Luke 11:5–13). This parable in Luke describes a man who persistently keeps knocking on a door until his friend gives him what he wanted. In the same way, we must keep asking and seeking for the Holy Spirit every day. We are as close to the Lord as we choose to be. The Bible warns that our anger, words, actions, or attitudes can grieve the Holy Spirit and give a stronghold to the enemy (Ephesians 4:26–32).

The Anointing of the Holy Spirit comes from God and not from other men or religious conferences. You can't order it online or buy it with money. Peter rebuked a magician named Simon. "Your silver perish with you, because you thought you could obtain the gift of God with money!" (Acts 8:20; see 8:9–24). I have seen people living in poverty because they have given all their money to a famous evangelist to get his "anointing." The Anointing is a free gift from God to those who love Him. The Lord pours out His Spirit on His followers who obey Him and walk with Him (Acts 5:32). Man has failed to obey God under the Law so in the New Covenant the Lord has poured out His Spirit to cause us to walk in obedience to Him. The Lord proclaims, "A new heart I will give you, and a new Spirit I will put within you; and I will take out of your flesh the heart of stone and give you a heart of flesh. And I will put My Spirit within you, and cause you to walk in my statutes" (Ezekiel 36:26–27). I pray, "Thank you for Your gift of the Holy Spirit. O Lord, let me always be filled with Thy Spirit. There is no life, no meaning, no understanding, and no purpose without Your Spirit. I love Thy Spirit. He will be with me Forever. Your Spirit makes all things Glorious!"

Truly, God is Good!

12 |
At the Feet of Jesus

For many years, I have sat at the feet of Jesus as He opened my heart to receive His teaching (Luke 24:13–53). I love His Word because it saves, delivers, redeems, and transforms me into His image. The Bible is a mirror through which I can know the Almighty God. I pray, "Jesus, let my heart and life always be consumed with a passion for Your teaching. I love to sit at Your feet and listen to Your instruction. Open my ears to hear Thy Voice and my eyes to see You. Thy Words are Life to my soul and healing to my body. They lead, guide, and comfort me in affliction. Your Word is my life. Teach me Thy Ways Forever". I have spent many wonderful hours in God's Presence as He revealed Himself to me through the Scriptures. Frequently, I have come to Jesus with burdens and sorrow, and He has Faithfully lifted me up into His Arms and comforted me through His Word. The Holy Spirit opened my eyes to see Him, and I was changed into His likeness from one degree of glory to another (2 Corinthians 3:18). Jesus put a passion in my heart to know Him, and as a baby in Christ, I drank of the pure milk of the Word until I grew up into maturity (1 Peter 2:2). Luke records a story of two sisters. Martha was distracted by serving, while Mary sat at the Lord's feet and listened to His teaching. Jesus commended Mary for choosing to spend her time listening to Him. I pray that the Father will always give me a heart like Mary to sit at the feet of Jesus and listen to Him teach (Luke 10:38–42). The Father has often lifted me up into His Presence and His Word has brought Life and comfort to me in the midst of great suffering. Thank you, Jesus, for Your Word! I love the journey, and I love the adventure of pursuing Him. God will always be a mystery. There will be a part of Him that will remain unrevealed and undiscovered. "The secret things belong to the Lord our God; but the things that are revealed belong to us and to our children forever, that we may do all the words of this law" (Deuteronomy 29:29). As long as I follow Jesus, He will always lead me to the Father (John 14:6). All I want is Him. My desires for this world fade away in God's Presence. Every day is an opportunity to draw closer to Him through His Scriptures. I love His Word! His Words are Life!

The Scriptures contain precious and very great promises with unlimited power to heal and transform our lives (2 Peter 1:3–4). God spoke His Word, and the universe was created. "By faith we understand that the world was created by the word of God, so that what is seen was made out of things which do not appear" (Hebrews 11:3). This same unlimited creative power is available to us through His Word. The infinite power is stored in His Word, and it is released by faith. In a similar way, one match can release the tremendous potential energy stored in gasoline. All things are possible to those who believe God's Word (Mark 9:23). Jesus proclaims to us, "It is the Spirit that gives life, the flesh is of no avail; the words that I have spoken to you are spirit and life" (John 6:63). In Ezekiel, we see a Vision of the Power of God's Word that brought Spirit and Life to God's people. God's Word raised them up from the grave to become a great Army (Ezekiel 37:1–14). All Scripture is Divinely Inspired by God. "All scripture is inspired by God and profitable for teaching, for reproof, for correction and for training in righteousness" (2 Timothy 3:16). The Father wrote every word in the Bible as His Love Letter to us. I have learned to let the Holy Spirit guide me to all Truth, and I no longer study the Scriptures in my own understanding (John 16:13). God is Spirit, and we can know Him only through the Spirit. No one comprehends the thoughts of God except the Spirit of God (1 Corinthians 2:9–13). The Word of God was written by the Holy Spirit, and only He can correctly interpret them (2 Peter 2:16–21). The Holy Spirit moved upon the writers of the Bible, and they wrote the perfect and complete Word of God. By His Sovereign Power, He has preserved this Word through the ages so that we might know Him. We are warned not to add to or take away from His Word (Revelation 22:18–19). The Word teaches us to allow the Anointing of the Spirit in us to guide us to all Truth. "I write this to you about those who would deceive you; but the anointing which you received from him abides in you and you have no need that any one should teach you; as his anointing teaches you about everything, and is true, and is no lie" (1 John 2:26–27).

I have chosen to come to the Light and be convicted of sin so that the Father could change me (John 3:19–21). I asked for the Sword of His Word to cut into my heart exposing sin, darkness, bitterness, pride, anger, and rebellion. "The word of God is living and active, sharper than any two-edged sword, piercing to the division of soul and spirit, of joints and marrow, and discerning the thoughts and intentions of the heart. and before him no creature is hidden, but all are open and laid bare to the eyes of him with whom we have to do" (Hebrews 4:12-13). I pray to Jesus, "Convict me of sin and wash them away in Your Blood. Burn away the flesh, remove the darkness and bring all things into subjection to Your authority. Expose all my hidden sins that are known only to You. Let Your Kingdom come and Your Will be done in my life. Set up Your Throne in my heart and Reign in me. I ask for Your Light to shine out of me to a world that is in darkness."

"Thank you, Lord, for preserving Your Holy Word so I might know You. Your Word is very precious beyond fine gold. Through Your Holy Scriptures, I have come to You and received Salvation, Forgiveness, and Eternal Life. I Love Thy Word beyond all the treasures of this world. Thy Word has filled my heart with Love and Hope. The Scriptures have brought Peace to my troubled mind and comfort to my soul. I will praise You Forever for Your Glorious Word."

Truly, God is Good!

13 | Prayer

Prayer Changes Us

Prayer changes us because it takes our focus off ourselves and our problems and causes us to look up to God. The Bible commands us not to worry but instead pray and put our trust in God. "Have no anxiety about anything, but in everything by prayer and supplication with thanksgiving let your requests be made known to God. And the peace of which passes all understanding, will keep your hearts and your minds in Christ Jesus" (Philippians 4:6–7). The Bible promises that the Lord will fill us with Peace when we stop worrying and begin to pray. We worry when we don't trust God with our problems, but instead try to "fix" them ourselves. I pray to the Father, "Please take away this fear and worry. I place it all in Your Hands because I trust Your Love. I am safe in Your Arms, and I rest in Your Presence. I need

not fear because You are with me. You Love me, and You will keep me from harm. I trust Your Love."

Listening

Prayer is communicating with God. It is a combination of talking and listening. I was Born Again in the mid-seventies, and I began a journey to know the Father. My first prayers were filled with my requests to God, but I gradually learned to be still and listen. I continued to pursue my relationship with Him until I became familiar with His Voice. My mind had been filled with voices of the flesh, the world, and the enemy. I began to realize that God had always been speaking to me, but that I was not yet able to hear Him. I pictured my mind as a room full of radios all playing at once. God's still small Voice was speaking to me in the midst of this confusion. I needed to "unplug" all the other voices so that I could hear the Lord. I learned to withdraw from this world, be still before the Lord and listen." The Father tells us to "be still and know that I am God" (Psalm 46:10). It is essential that we learn to be still and commune with God in the secret place of His Presence. His sheep are able to follow Him because they have learned to hear His Voice (John 10:1–4, 27). It is imperative that we keep seeking God until we learn to recognize His Voice. In the early years of my walk with the Lord, I was unfamiliar with God's Voice just as Samuel was in his youth (1 Samuel 3:1–14). Samuel had been raised in the Temple, but He "did not know the Lord and the word of the Lord had not yet been revealed to him" (1 Samuel 3:7). The Lord called Samuel several times before he learned to recognize the Father's Voice. We go to Church and read His Word, but do we know His Voice?

God is Spirit, and He often speaks to us through His Spirit, but do we hear Him? In Heaven, we will communicate exclusively by the Spirit. On earth, we need to begin to learn this Heavenly form of communication. In Revelation, Jesus told John to send the same message to all seven Churches in Asia. "He that has an ear, let him hear what the Spirit says to the Churches" (Revelation 2:7, 11, 17, 29; 3:6, 13, 22. Jesus was exhorting the Church to become listeners. My primary goal in prayer is to enter into God's Presence and spend all day in fellowship with Him. Sin separates us from God, so I often begin by confessing my sins and asking for forgiveness. I then lay all my burdens and worries at His feet. I continue to seek God until I leave behind this world and enter into His Presence. (James 4:8). I am then quiet and listen for the Voice of His Spirit.

The Prayer Closet

We need to find a place to separate from this world and be alone with God. Moses pitched the Tent of Meeting outside the camp for people to seek the Lord. "Now Moses used to take the tent and pitch it outside the camp, far from the camp; and he called it the tent of meeting. And every one who sought the Lord would go out to the tent of meeting, which was outside the camp" (Exodus 32:7–8). Today, we don't use tents to seek God, but we still need to separate ourselves from all things and begin to focus on God. Jesus teaches us to find a secret place(a prayer closet) to be alone with the Father. "But when you pray go into your room and shut the door and pray to your Father who is in secret; and your Father who sees in secret will reward you" (Matthew 6:6). The prayer closet is a place where we separate from everything, and we concentrate all of our hearts and minds on the Lord. Jesus is our example of how to pray. He often spent all night alone with the Father to prepare Himself for the next day of ministry. "And after he had dismissed the crowds, he went up into the hills by himself to pray" (Matthew 14:23). Again, "in these days he went out into the hills to pray, and all night he continued in prayer to God" (Luke 6:12). Jesus needed to draw strength from the Father every day. How much more do we need to pray!

Help in Time of Need

I have learned to come to the Throne of Grace to receive help in times of distress. "For we have not a high priest who is unable to sympathize with our weaknesses, but one who in every respect has been tempted as we are, yet without sinning. Let us then with confidence draw near to the throne of grace, that we may receive mercy and find grace to help in time of need" (Hebrews 4:15–16). He is able to understand our weaknesses because He has been tempted in every way while on this earth and yet without sinning. I have learned to humble myself and cry out to God for many hours at a time. Jesus drew His strength from the Father through prayer. He offered prayers with loud cries to God who was able to save Him from death, and He was heard for His godly fear (Hebrews 5:7). We must cry out to God with our whole hearts and give to Him all our burdens and pain (Matthew 11:28–30). I am open and honest with God and tell Him exactly how I feel. Without hesitation, I express to Jesus my anger, fear, worry, frustration, and confusion. I need not be afraid because He already knows my heart. Sometimes, my burdens are so heavy that I spend all night in prayer until the yoke of oppression from the enemy is broken. In our weakness, we need to allow the Holy Spirit to help us to pray according to the will of God (Romans 8:26–27).

Pray Without Ceasing

The Word commands us to pray without ceasing. (Luke 18.1-8). I seek to pray at all times and stay in fellowship with the Father. It is important to develop a habit of praying from the moment that we awake until the time that we sleep. We need Christ at all times and apart from Him we can do nothing. (John 15.5). My goal is to stay in continual communication with God while I am eating, driving in the car, shopping and at work. I fall short every day because I often let the world and the flesh draw me away from the Lord. My spirit is willing but my flesh is weak. Jesus is the only one to walk perfectly with the Father because He always sought to do God's will and not His own. (John 6.38). Everything in life becomes Glorious when we walk with Him in the Spirit. The times that we walk alone will pass away, but the works that Christ does through us are Eternal because He is Eternal.

Come to Jesus

We can come to Him at any time through the new and living way, which Christ has given us through His Blood (Hebrews 10:19–22). When Jesus died on the Cross, the Veil into the Holy of Holies was torn from top to bottom. In the Old Covenant, only the High Priest could enter beyond the curtain, and this was only once per year. Through Christ, we can enter into His Presence every day, but do we come? I press on to know Him with the upward call of God in Christ (Philippians 3:7–14). I am not satisfied with knowing about Him from afar. I desire to draw near to Him until I dwell in His Presence Forever. God has put it into my heart to seek Him like Moses. Moses sought God's Presence, Glory and His Ways (Exodus 33:12-23). The Father gave him the desires of his heart, and He spoke to Moses as a friend (Exodus 33:11). I know of no higher goal in life. "Take delight in the Lord, and he will give you the desires of your heart" (Psalm 37:4). I am thankful for the many times that God has graciously allowed me to rest in His Presence. He wants to spend time with us because He loves us. I pray, "Lord let me never be too busy to spend time with You. Please keep me from living in the fast pace of this world, but teach me to slow down and rest in Your Arms. You always make time for me; let me always make time for You. I love those days I have spent with You. They are more precious to me than all the gold in the world. I cherish the years I have walked with You. Thank you, Jesus!"

Truly, God is Good!

14 | The Call to Live by Faith

In the mid-seventies, God called me to separate myself from this present world and come follow Him. In obedience, I left behind my family, my career, and my homeland. Like Abraham, I went out not knowing where I was going (Hebrews 11:8). God called me out of this world, and Heaven was now my home. I became a stranger and exile on this earth, looking forward to a new land where Righteousness dwells (Hebrews 11:13–16). By faith, I have walked with God for forty-six years knowing that my home was in God's Presence and not on this earth. I have never been content with my life in this world, but I have been content with Him. God has been faithful to me as I "pitched my tent" in this life, seeking Him with all my heart. He met with me on the mountain tops and carried me through the deepest valleys of suffering. I have feared no evil in the valley of the shadow of death for He was with me. Like Peter, I learned to look up to Jesus by faith and walk above the water (the evil and hate of this world) (Matthew 14:28–33). I sometimes become afraid when I look down at my circumstances, and I sink into the darkness of this world. I then cry out to Jesus, and He has been faithful to reach out His Hand and lift me back up into Heavenly places. I have endured the

From the rising of the sun to its setting the LORD"S name is to be praised. Psalm 113:3

trials of my life by seeing the Lord's Glory in all things. Jesus is the Good Shepherd, and He has led me safely through every storm.

Those who live by faith are Blessed by the Lord, and they become like a tree planted by water (the Holy Spirit) that bears fruit in difficult times. These believers have their "roots" in the Holy Spirit and are full of Joy, Peace, and Love in all circumstances. They draw their strength from Christ and have Victory, even in tribulation. Those who put their trust in the flesh become like a dry shrub in the desert without hope. They are defeated by every trial and temptation, and they will never see the Goodness and Blessings of God (Jeremiah 17:5–8). Are we living by faith and bearing the fruit of the Spirit in times of tribulation? The Word teaches, "This is the victory that overcomes the world, our faith" (1 John 5.4). The Father has called us to live by faith and trust Him in these last days of darkness. The details of God's Plan are often hidden from our sight. He is like a Divine artist who is painting a masterpiece with our lives. During the journey, the outcome is not visible to our eyes, but in the end, we will see God's "painting" completed, and it will all make sense. Joseph received two dreams from God that he would be a leader over his family, but it took thirteen years of suffering before the fulfillment came to pass. He lived by faith through the betrayal of his brothers, slavery, and prison. "His feet were hurt with fetters, his neck was put in a collar of iron; until what he had said came to pass the word of the Lord tested him" (Psalm 105:18–19). God's Word was fulfilled to him at the age of thirty when he became governor of Egypt. Looking back over those years, he could see God's hand in all of it. Many years later, Joseph told his brothers that it had been God who had sent him to Egypt and not them (Genesis 45:4–8). God's Plan was to preserve many lives through Joseph. He also said to his brothers, "As for you, you meant evil against me; but God meant it for good, to bring it about that many people should be kept alive, as they are today" (Genesis 50:20). As I look back upon my life, I realize that God has truly worked in everything for good (Romans 8.28). The Father is in complete control of our lives even when we don't understand His Plan. I have learned to live by faith and not lean to my own understanding as I wait on Him (Proverbs 3:5–8).

As believers, we will be tested in this world by tragedy, suffering, death of a loved one, sickness, and financial problems. If our faith is in Christ, then we will still be standing at the end of the trials. If our faith is in anything else, we will fall (Matthew 7:24–27). The Father allows suffering to test our faith and to determine if it is genuine. True faith, when it has been tested, becomes as precious as gold (1 Peter 1:6–7). Our lives glorify God when we endure trials and afflictions by faith. I pray, "O Lord, give me the Grace to keep the faith and finish the race set before me!" (2 Timothy 4:7). There is a story of a young boy in a hurricane that illustrates simple childlike faith. He was afraid of the wind that was blowing violently outside of his home. The young boy hid between the legs of his father and asked if they were going to die. The father told him that they would be all right, and the boy went to bed and slept through the largest hurricane in the history of that city. The son trusted the words of his father. We must also learn to trust in the Father's words and rest in Him. He will protect us, and He will never forsake us. I pray, "O Lord, I rest in Your arms in the midst of the great storm of these last days. I am safe in Your Presence. Help me to always see through eyes of faith and trust You in all things. I know You are with me, even when I can't see You. I will not fear as I walk through this valley of the shadow of death for You are with me. I know this by faith. Your Word promises that You will never leave me or forsake me (Hebrews 13:5). I trust Your Word. I trust You. You are my Heavenly Father. I am Your child. I trust Your Love."

Truly, God is Good!

15
Spiritual Warfare

The Spiritual Battle

    We are in the final battle at the end of this age, and God is raising up the Church as His Army to prepare for the return of Christ and His Kingdom. The enemy is trying to oppose God's plan by making war against the Saints, but he will not prevail because Jesus is the King of kings and the Lord of lords (Philippians 2:10–11). The devil is full of wrath because he knows his time is short (Revelation 12:12). We must stand in the Power of the Holy Spirit as we wrestle with these principalities of darkness. The Lord has given us the Armor of God which is empowered by the Holy Spirit to help us to stand against the forces of evil in these last days. We walk in Victory as long as we stay in fellowship with the Lord and walk in the Spirit. When we walk alone without Christ, we become easy prey for the enemy. The Sword of the Spirit is our only offensive weapon. Jesus used the Word of God to defeat the temptations of the enemy in the wilderness.

Then Jesus told his disciples, "If any man would come after me, let him deny himself and take up his cross and follow me.
Matthew 16.24

He spoke God's Word to overcome the lies of the devil (Ephesians 6:10–18, Luke 4:1–13). Jesus is coming as King with the Armies of Heaven (the Church), and He has commanded us to be strong and of great courage to stand against the darkness of this world.

We have been called to live in the close of this present age and in the dawn of the new age of Christ. Satan and His army continue to fight against the coming of God's Kingdom, and the great move of the Holy Spirit in the end-times often called the Latter Rain. God poured out His Spirit (the Early Rain) in Acts to empower the Church to spread His Word to the world. He will soon pour out His Spirit (the Latter Rain) in these last days to prepare His Bride for His return. The outpouring of the Spirit will refine, sanctify, and gather His Church for His Coming. Satan will resist God's Plan, but he will fail. When we look at this world through our natural eyes, it appears that Satan is in control, and that everything is getting worse. He is a liar, and he is deceiving the world to think that he rules. When we walk by faith, we see that the whole world is filled with the Glory of God, and that Christ rules (Isaiah 6:3). Jesus will destroy the devil, and his kingdom with His appearance and His coming. He will Reign on earth Forever (Daniel 2:3–45; Daniel 7).

During my seven-year illness, the Lord began to reveal to me the spiritual world that is usually hidden behind the veil. In the midst of the physical suffering, I was called to live in the Spirit in Heavenly places. I became aware of the cloud of witnesses—the saints who had died in Christ during the past ages (Hebrews 12:1). The Father showed me that there was a Heavenly battle between the Armies of God and the armies of the evil one that affects the events upon this earth. We either serve God and walk in the Spirit, or we will serve the prince of this world and his spiritual powers of darkness (1 John 5:19, Ephesians 6:10–18, Luke 4:5–8). The Church is called to go forth in the power of the Spirit and spread the Good News of the Gospel of Grace to those who are lost. The enemy seeks to resist this Army of God with all his forces of darkness, but the Spirit of God in the Church is greater than the spirit of this world (1 John 4:4). Someday, we will go through this veil, and all things will be revealed to us, but in this life, we are called to walk by faith and proclaim God's Love to all people.

Persecution

I have experienced persecution from family, friends, and other Christians since I have decided to follow Christ. The Word warns that "all those who desire to live a godly life in Christ Jesus will be persecuted" (2 Timothy 3:12). Persecution will be experienced by all those who truly follow Christ. Many were jealous of my relationship with the Father. I sought to walk in peace and safety in God's Presence, but I was frequently under attack from the enemy. I have cried out to God in the midst of trials, and He has rescued me and sheltered me in the safety of His Presence far from the forces of evil.

The enemy will often attack us through family members, friends, and fellow Christians. "A man's foes will be those of his own household" (Matthew 10:36; see 10:16–23), (John 15:18–25). The world hated Jesus without cause, and many will hate us because He has chosen us out of this world. Jesus warns, "If the world hates you, know that it has hated me before it hated you. If you were of the world, the world would love its own; but because you are not of the world, but I chose you out of the world, therefore the world hates you" (John 15:18–19). "We know we are of God, and the whole world lies in the power of the evil one" (1 John 5:19). God's Word is clear that we will be hated by all for the name of Christ (Matthew 10:22). The Scriptures warn that the devil's followers disguise themselves as servants of righteousness (2 Corinthians 11:12–15). I have been hated, excluded, and cast out by many who called themselves Christians, but by faith, I continue to follow Christ. God's Word tells us that we are blessed when we are persecuted. "Blessed are you when men hate you, and when they exclude you and revile you, and cast out your name as evil, on account of the Son of Man! Rejoice in that day and leap for joy, for behold, your reward is great in heaven, for so their fathers did to the prophets" (Luke 6:22–23).

I have spent many years crying out to God in the midst of intense spiritual warfare. The enemy resists all those who truly serve God, and like David, I continue to ask the Lord to deliver me from my enemies. I have prayed, "Lord, I long to dwell in the shadow of Thy wings in the safety of Thy Presence. Hide me from my enemies and from the evil of this present world. Take me to a place where there is no rejection for me, where people know me and accept me for who You made me to be. Remove me from the false accusation, condemnation, judgment, and jealousy. Deliver me from my enemies who hate me and seek to destroy me. They hate my innocent heart, my love for You, and my love for all Your creation. Let me dwell in Thy Presence Forever far away from hate and evil. I seek to behold Thy Glory and Thy Beauty throughout Eternity. Let me live in safety where no one can steal my life, afflict me, or seek to drive me into discouragement." David writes, "Let me dwell in thy tent forever. Oh, to be safe under the shelter of thy wings" (Psalm 61:4). David often prayed to God for deliverance, "My times are in thy hand; deliver me from the hand of my enemies and persecutors! Let thy face shine on thy servant; save me in thy steadfast love!" (Psalm 31:15–16).

I prayed in tribulation, "Restore to me the years the locust have taken (Joel 2.25). The evil doers that sought to steal my life, body, and my mind, but I am still in Your Hands. You know all the times that I walked with you in Your Presence. The days I spent with you are not lost; they are written in Your Book. Thou hast saved my soul. The enemies have sought to steal my life, but Thou hast preserved it Forever. You will restore all that the enemy sought to steal from me, with even greater Glory. Lord, You have shown me a Vision of Heaven, and You will place me there with You Forever. The enemy has sought to erase the memory of my life, but You would not allow it. Truly, God has protected me and preserved me for His Kingdom. Thank you, Jesus, for Your protection and Mercy in this great spiritual battle at the end of this age. I need not fear, for nothing can separate me from Your Love." If God is for us, who can be against us? (Romans 8.31–39). Jesus has already defeated sin and the devil on the Cross. Let us go forth by faith and walk in this Victory!

God's Model for Victory

The Word of God gives us a beautiful account of successful spiritual warfare in 2 Chronicles 20. In this passage, three armies came out to destroy the people of Israel and King Jehoshaphat led his people to seek God, pray, and worship Him. In humility, they confessed their weakness and asked God to deliver them. As the people sought God, He spoke through His prophet not to be afraid because the battle is the Lord's. They were told not to fight but only stand and see His Victory. The people obeyed and worshiped God with all their hearts. God caused the three enemy armies to fight against themselves and not one of them survived. The Israelites spent three days collecting the spoil with great rejoicing. Truly, the battle is the Lord's. This passage gives us a model for true spiritual victory. We must humble ourselves, seek God's help, and let Him give us the Victory. Jesus has already defeated the enemies on the cross, and we must learn to stand in His Victory in the last days of darkness.

Truly, God is Good!

16 | Visions

For over forty-four years, God has given me Visions about the coming His Kingdom and His Rule on this earth. God states that in these last days that He will "pour out my spirit upon all flesh, and your sons and your daughters shall prophesy, and your young men shall see visions, and your old men shall dream dreams" (Acts 2:7). The Word of God is clear: Visions and Prophecies are a result of being filled with the Spirit. God frequently reveals His Plan to His people through his prophets (Amos 3:7). The Father has chosen to give me several Visions that I have included in this passage. For the past forty-four years, I have learned to rest and wait on God who will accomplish all things according to His will. From my viewpoint, I have waited a long time, but I must realize that from God's perspective, a thousand years is like one day (2 Peter 3:8). I have recorded these Visions as the Father revealed them to me. I will let God bring them to pass in His time and according to His Sovereign Plan. He has called me to live by faith and walk with Him each day until all things are fulfilled. When I sometimes get discouraged as I wait, the Lord answers me, "Write the vision; make it plain upon tablets so he may run who reads it. For still. the vision awaits its time; it hastens to the end; it will not lie. If it seems slow, wait for it; I will surely come, it will not delay. Behold, he whose soul is not upright in him shall fail. But the righteous shall live by his faith." (Habakkuk. 2:2–4).

Church Rising Out of the Rubble (Mid-70s)

God's first Vision to me was of a beautiful shining crystal structure (the Church) rising out of dark rubble. He showed me that the true remnant of the Church was going to rise up out of the rubble of the apostate lukewarm Church.

God's Call to Me in 1977

In 1977, I was driving to Church on a Wednesday night, and suddenly, I was in the Shekinah Glory of God. I looked up, and I saw hundreds of Angels looking down in ascending circular balconies that reached up to Heaven. I was told to take off my shoes because I was standing on Holy Ground. God spoke three things to me: "Thou are my chosen one," "Thou shalt bless all the nations," and "I am God." The Father revealed to me that He would take away my life and then give it back again. He gave me a sign by crippling my hands and then healing them. This word was fulfilled several years later in 1981 when I went through a seven-year near-terminal illness. I saw Paul in a spiritual body, and The Father told me that like Paul I had been called to suffer. He also stated that the time of the Gentiles was nearing an end, and the time of the Jews was soon to begin (see Romans (11:25–26). I drove to Church after this Vision, filled with great Joy, and I was told by members of the Church that I appeared to be glowing with God's Glory. (Exodus 34:29–35). The first song that we sang began with these words: "I saw the Lord and He was high and lifted up and His train filled the Temple" (Isaiah 6:1–5).

Vision of Jesus on a White Throne

The Lord has given me this Vision in the mid-eighties and in the mid-nineties. In the second Vision, I was worshiping the Lord for about two and a half hours at a crusade. The Holy Spirit was so strong in the building that many were healed and I saw a Vision of Jesus on a White Throne in the middle of the auditorium. When I left the arena, I could see a wall of demonic darkness about ten feet from the building. Evil had been driven away by the Presence of God. We live in a world of darkness, but God's Spirit and Power is greater than evil (1 John 4:4).

Vision of Paul and the Modern Church

In this Vision, I saw a man covered in blood from a beating, sitting in a prison cell. He was released and began to walk down a street. The scene then changed to a modern Church with a large beautiful building. People were arriving in their nice cars, wearing fancy clothes. Everyone was smiling as they were greeted at the doorway of the Church. The worship music was beautiful. The scene switched back to the man walking the streets with old torn clothes. He arrived at the large Church during their beautiful ceremony. The man was "greeted" at the door by security and removed from the property. The service continued as the Pastor stood up and began to preach from a book that Paul had written. In this Vision, the man that he had removed from the Church was Paul. The Holy Spirit told me that the modern Church had become so far removed from the True Gospel that they had just kicked out Paul (or Jesus) from their service.

Vision of Second Coming of Christ: 1996

I was on the front lawn of a Church when the Lord gave me a Vision of the Second Coming of Christ. I was filled with the Holy Spirit in a very powerful way, and it seemed like I was being raised up with Christ. The Power of the Holy Spirit seemed too great for this earthly body to contain. I believe that this was a glimpse of the Glory of Christ's Second Coming when He will transform our earthly bodies into a Heavenly body like His. Come, Lord Jesus, Come!

Vision of a Worldwide Ministry (mid-90s)

I was at a Church Revival when I saw a Vision of the earth that looked like a globe. In this Vision, I was moving over the face of the earth to all nations. I believed that I had been called to minister to the world.

Vision of a Large Auditorium Full of People

Twice, the Lord has given me this Vision. Both times, I stepped into a large auditorium full of thousands of people. The Holy Spirit was very powerful and moving through the crowd. I also introduced my wife to the people. In this Vision, God's Spirit was using me as His vessel to touch many lives in a very powerful way. Many people were being saved and healed as the Holy Spirit worked great miracles.

Vision of the Healing Power of the Spirit

In this Vision, I walked into a medical facility, and the Power of the Holy Spirit flowed through me to heal many people. I believed that the Lord was showing me a Vision of the great outpouring of the Spirit in the Latter Rain.

Vision of the Open Door (Mid-Nineties)

I saw a Vision of an open door into Heaven, and Jesus called me up to come up to Him into Heavenly places. This Vision was similar to John's Vision in chapter 4 of Revelation. The Father told me to read and preach the Word, pray and worship in Heaven before His Throne by the Spirit. When we walk with Him our words, prayer and worship becomes very powerful. He showed me that the Latter Rain was coming soon as a great outpouring of the Holy Spirit to prepare the Bride for the coming of the Bridegroom. Jesus would come for her as the Great King full of Power and great Glory.

Vision of the Latter Rain (1997)

I wrote an account of this Vision: "Last night, I was caught up in the Spirit to God's throne. God's mouth was open and ready to speak the command to send forth the Glory of the Holy Spirit upon the earth. The trumpet was ready to sound. I said, 'O, Lord let it be now.' God replied that He was ready to speak the command, but it will be in His perfect time. He also said that He is pouring out great Power and Glory so that every knee shall bow before Him. Those who hate Jesus will bow before Him in terror. Those who love Jesus will come to Him, be filled with His Glory, and be changed into His likeness. The believers will be joined to Jesus as a Bride without spot or blemish. God is about to pour out more of His Glory through His Spirit on this earth than has ever been seen since the beginning of time. Through His Grace, the Spirit will be poured out into earthen vessels (His Church). This world will end with a shout of Victory as when the Israelites shouted on the seventh day, and the walls of Jericho fell down. We are entering the seventh day of rest: the final Victory!"

God also revealed to me that I am like a desert flower, which He has prepared for many years, waiting for His Glory to come and the Latter Rain to fall. There will be a heavy downpour of rain (the Spirit) when Jesus comes to glorify the Father. I was born on this earth to glorify Him in the last days of the great outpouring of His Spirit.

Vision of God's Kingdom Coming

In the past several years, God has shown me a Vision of the seventh trumpet when the kingdom of this world will become the Kingdom of God (Revelation 11:15). We are living at the end of this age of the kingdom of darkness and the beginning of the age of the Reign of Christ in His Kingdom on this earth with His Church. Satan and the powers of darkness will wage war against Christ, but He has already won the Victory on the Cross. We are about to see the reality of this Victory on this earth. We've now groan in travail for Christ to come and set us free from bondage to sin and death. We long for Him to Reign on this earth and destroy the kingdom of darkness. We seek for all things to be subjected to Him. The Spirit and Bride say, "Come" (Revelation 22:17).

God's Word for These Last Days

A word has come forth from God that all believers from the beginning of time have waited for. The Lord says that He has waited so long for this time to show Himself fully to His people. He proclaims that no longer will there be darkness, bondage, fear, suffering, and pain. God will now be revealed in His Church, and He will dwell with them Forever. The old will pass away, and God will make all things new. Hallelujah!

For a short time, Satan was given power over the Church to purify us. Judgment begins in the Household of God, but Satan's time is over, and his end is near. Satan and his people will wither like the grass in the hot sun when God fully shines out of His Church. God created us not for this world or for Satan to oppress, but God's plan is to Bless us with Eternal Life in His Presence. We will live with Him in a New Land, which He has prepared for us. The Throne of God and of the Lamb will be in the midst of His people. God will dwell with us Forever. We will see His Face. Amen! Hallelujah!

The Bridegroom Comes

Behold, the Bridegroom comes full of Passion and Glory. Break the chains of darkness and open your eyes to see Your King in His Glory. He will clothe you with fine linen (the righteous deeds of His people) and embrace you with His Love. You will no longer be afraid, for the Bridegroom will keep you safe in His Arms. When Jesus removes evil from His Kingdom, then the Bride will shine bright with His Glory. "The Son of man will send His angels, and they will gather out of his Kingdom all causes of sin and all evildoers, and throw them into the furnace of fire; there men will weep and gnash their teeth. Then the righteous will shine like the sun in the kingdom of their Father" (Matthew 13:41–43). "They will see the Son of man coming on the clouds of heaven with power and great glory; and he will send out his angels with a loud trumpet call, and they will gather his elect from the four winds, from one end of heaven to the other" Matthew 24:30–31). Jesus will soon destroy all the kingdoms of this earth that rage against Him. He will sit on the Throne and bring all things in subjection to Himself for He is the King of kings and the Lord of lords (1 Corinthians 15:24–26). Every knee shall bow and every tongue will confess that He is Lord. (Philippians 2:9–11). God promises that He will place His people in the safety of His Presence that they have longed for. Their reward is waiting for them, and no one will steal their crowns. Jesus is calling His Church out of the kingdom of this world (Egypt) into a new Heavenly Land. Jesus is shouting, "Let my people go," and the devil (Pharaoh) is resisting the Plan of God. The enemy seeks to keep God's people in slavery to sin and in bondage under the oppression of this present darkness. They cry out for a deliverer. Behold, He comes to deliver His people from slavery and take them to His Heavenly Kingdom. He will set His people free by the power of His Blood and by the great outpouring of His Holy Spirit to gather His Church. Behold the Savior comes and He will break their chains of deception and bondage to sin. He will place His Church in the safety of His Presence Forever. Jesus will destroy the destroyers of this earth and give us a Kingdom that will never be destroyed. He will Reign with His Saints Forever. Amen!

My Prayer for the Church

"O Lord pour out Your Spirit upon Your people and fill our hearts with a passion to know You. Let Your people fall in love with Jesus, and let His Presence fill their souls. Call Your people out of Egypt (the world), and draw them to You Forever. Break the power of the enemy and the bondage of slavery to sin. Let them lay down their idols and bow down to the One True Living God who loves His people. By Your Grace, cause Your Church to rise up with the power of the Spirit and become an exceedingly great Army. Send forth Your Angels to gather Your Bride from the four corners of Heaven. Let them come together as one people united in Your Love. May Your Spirit draw them out of this world to sit with You in Heavenly places. Call them out of the kingdom of this world to Your Glorious Kingdom. Purify their hearts that the Light of Jesus may shine forth out of His Bride. Remove from us the love for this world and replace it with a pure and holy devotion to You. Pour out a Baptism of Fire to burn away our flesh by the power of the Holy Spirit. Make us a Bride full of Holiness and without blemish awaiting the coming of the Bridegroom. Let us be clothed with the Righteousness of Christ. Sanctify and cleanse us with the washing of Your Holy Word. Lord, make us ready as a Bride prepared for Her Husband."

"The Spirit and the Bride say, 'Come'" (Revelation 22:17).

> "And the kingdom and the dominion and the greatness of the kingdoms under the whole heaven shall be given to the people of the saints of the Most High; their kingdom shall be an

everlasting kingdom, and all dominions shall serve and obey them" (Daniel 7:27).

Truly, God is Good!

17 | Forgiveness

The Good News of the Gospel is that Jesus bore our sins, took our punishment on the Cross, and offers Forgiveness and Eternal Life to those who believe in Him. We deserve death, but the Father in His Mercy has chosen to give us Grace. "For the wages of sin is death, but the free gift of God is Eternal life in Christ Jesus our Lord" (Romans 6:23). As Christians, we accept this Amazing Grace from the Father, but we then sometimes struggle with the commandment to forgive others. I have sometimes refused to forgive others, and bitterness and anger filled my heart. My heart became cold and hard. I looked into the mirror, and I didn't like the person whom I had become. I cried out to God to heal my heart and set me free from bitterness. I have learned to forgive immediately and release the anger before it becomes sin. "Be angry but do not sin; do not let the sun go down on your anger, and give no opportunity for the devil" (Ephesians 4:26–27). The ways of the enemy are bitterness and anger, while the ways of God are Mercy and Love.

The Three Steps of Forgiveness (See Matthew 18:23–35)

In this parable, the King (God) extends Mercy to a man who owed Him a large amount of money (or sin). The Lord forgave all his debt (sin), but this man then showed no mercy to a fellow servant who owed him a small amount of money. The Lord, in His anger, delivered this man over to jailors and tormentors. The lesson of the story is clear: the Father shows us unconditional Mercy and Forgiveness, and we are commanded to show that same mercy to others. How often have we been in torment and misery because we refuse to forgive?

God's Forgiveness to Us

Forgiveness begins as a gift from God made possible through the death of Jesus on the Cross. "For God so loved the world that he gave his only Son, that whoever believes in him should not perish but have eternal life" (John 3:16). The Word of God promises that the Lord will forgive every sin that we confess. "If we confess our sins, he is faithful and just and will forgive our sins and cleanse us from all unrighteousness" (1 John 1:9). We are saved by Grace through faith and not by works. "For by grace we are saved through faith; and this is not your own doing, it is the gift of God, not because of works, lest any man should boast" (Ephesians 2:8–9). God's Forgiveness is so complete that He doesn't even remember our sins. "I will remember their sins and their misdeeds no more" (Hebrews 10:17). Every confessed sin is nailed to the Cross and forgotten (Colossians 2:13–15).

The Word teaches that all of us were on the road to destruction, but God in His great Love extended Mercy to us through Christ. The Scriptures describe our condition before Christ: dead in sin, following the course of this world and the prince of this world. We lived in the lusts and passions of our flesh, and by nature, we were children destined for wrath (Ephesians 2:1–10). We did nothing to deserve this Salvation. It is all a gift from God through the death of Jesus on the Cross. Thank you, Jesus! The Blood of Christ forgives our sins, reconciles us to God, and gives us Eternal Life. We cannot earn our way to Heaven or attain righteousness by good works. There are many religions in this world that teach many paths to "righteousness," but none of them can deal with the problem of sin. Sin can only be removed through Jesus.

Forgive Ourselves

The Father has forgiven all of our sin, and He commands us to let go of the guilt and shame of the past. The Lord has forgotten our sins. Why do we still remember them? It is impossible to follow Christ while we are looking back to the past. "No one who puts his hand to the plow and looks back is fit for the kingdom of God" (Luke 9:62). Jesus met Saul on the road to Damascus and revealed to him that he had been killing and persecuting the Church of God. Jesus called him to build up the Church that he had once tried to destroy. Paul could have let his guilt overcome him, live in the past, and refuse to follow Christ. He realized that the past cannot be changed, and that he couldn't bring back to life all those who had been murdered. He decided to leave his sins at the Cross and follow Christ. Paul accepted God's Grace, and the Lord used him in a mighty way to save many lives. Jesus is calling us to lay aside every burden and sin and run the race set before us (Hebrews 12:1–2). Guilt and shame causes some people to feel unworthy of God's Goodness and Blessing in their lives. They felt more comfortable being miserable, and some have returned to their self- destructive lifestyles. It is true that we don't deserve God's Forgiveness; it is a gift from God. I have seen guilt lead people to addiction, chronic illnesses, severe mental illness, and even suicide and death. Let us give our burdens to Christ and let Him set us free (John 8:31–32).

Forgive Others

The Father showed amazing Mercy to us when He forgave all of our sins, and He commands us to show this Mercy to others. We ask the Lord to forgive our sins, and then we sometimes want judgment and punishment for those who have harmed us. The Word warns, "But if you do not forgive men their trespasses, neither will your Father forgive your trespasses" (Matthew 6:14). The Father's Agape Love in us helps us to love our enemies and pray for those who despitefully use us. We must seek God's Grace and strength to help us forgive others (Hebrews 4:15–16). Jesus is our example when He chose to forgive all of us while nailed to the Cross as a Righteous man. Jesus cried out in the midst of injustice and intense pain, "Father, forgive them; for they know not what they do" (Luke 23:34). Jesus has often helped me with the Grace to forgive when my pain seemed to overwhelm me. Many people are miserable because they carry around anger and bitterness from the past. Unforgiveness torments us and eats away our well being like cancer. Bitterness can cause physical and mental illness and can even lead to death. "See to it that no one fails to obtain the grace of God; that no 'root of bitterness' spring up and cause trouble, and by it the many become defiled" (Hebrews 12:15). Forgiveness releases us from the power of the past and sets us free to follow Christ. I pray, "Lord, give me the strength to always forgive those who have harmed me. Please don't let my heart become hard with bitterness and anger. Lord, set me free from the chains of the past so I may run the race set before me. Father, give me the heart of Jesus to always love and show mercy to others."

18 | Born Again

Jesus teaches that we must be Born Again of the Spirit. "Truly, truly, I say to you, unless one is born of water and the Spirit, he cannot enter the kingdom of God" (John 3:5. See 3:1–8). But what does the term Born Again mean? Is it simply standing up or walking forward in a Church and saying a sinner's prayer? Jesus cautions that not everyone who prays a sinner's prayer is actually saved. "Not everyone who says to me, 'Lord, Lord,' shall enter the kingdom of heaven but he who does the will of my Father who is in heaven'" (Matthew 7:21). We are not saved by works—by Grace, we are saved through faith (Ephesians 2:8)—but the works are the evidence of the faith that is in our hearts. The Bible describes a true Born Again experience in Acts 2. Peter preached a sermon, which brought conviction to a crowd of over three thousand Israelites. They were cut to the heart and came to the disciples, asking what to do (Acts 2:37). The Word is clear, "No one can come to Me unless the Father who sent me draws him" (John 6:44). During my early years in ministry, I used to attempt to draw people to Christ through any means possible. I preached an easy wide gate Gospel so many could enter. The Lord warned me to not to mislead people into thinking that they were saved when they were not truly Born Again of the Spirit. The Holy Spirit instructed me that He must draw the lost, bring conviction, and lead them to true repentance. I now let the Spirit do the drawing and try to keep myself out of it. The Holy Spirit draws, convicts, and saves us. Salvation is a work of God from the beginning to the end. Jesus taught that Salvation is impossible with man, but with God, all things are possible (Mark 10:26–27).

Blessed is he whom Thou dost choose to dwell in Thy courts!
Psalm 65.4

The Word of God reveals to us several steps for a new believer to take when they come to Christ. We must Repent (Acts 2:38), be Born Again (John 3:5), be Water Baptized (Acts 2:39; Romans 6:4), and be Baptized in the Holy Spirit (Acts 2:38–39).

Fruits of Repentance

True repentance is more than mere words, and it brings about a complete and total change in direction of our lives. We repent when we decide to leave the wide path of destruction and have chosen to follow Christ on the narrow path of life (Matthew 7:13–14). The Bible warns that there must be fruits of repentance (Matthew 3:7–10). In the Scriptures, Jesus preached repentance to His disciples, and they responded immediately by dropping their nets, leaving their businesses and their families (Matthew 4:17–22). The wide and easy Gospel leaves out the Cross and the cost of following Christ. The lukewarm dead Church produces stillborn babies that bear no fruit. Their lives remain unchanged because they were "saved" by religion but not by the Holy Spirit. The Bible describes the fruit being Born Again in Acts 2. The Holy Spirit spoke through Peter after Pentecost, and three thousand people repented and gave their lives to Christ. They had come from many parts of the world for the Festival, but they all chose to stay in Jerusalem to devote themselves to the Word of God, prayer, and fellowship (Acts 2:42–47). Their hearts were immediately changed, and they were filled with a passion to know Christ, study His Word, pray, and fellowship with other believers. When the Almighty God who created the universe comes into our lives, there will be an immediate, dramatic, and visible difference. These converts were a new creation in Christ and left their old lives behind (2

Corinthians 5:17). They were not yet perfect or mature, but they had been transformed by the work of the Holy Spirit. Young Christians grow up quickly on the milk of God's Word (1 Peter 2:2). As a young believer, the Father had imparted to me a seemingly endless passion to know my Heavenly Father, study His Word, talk with Him in prayer, and to worship Him. Salvation is completely a work of God's Grace and not a result of our own efforts. The passion of the Holy Spirit that was ignited in me over forty-six years ago still burns bright inside my heart. Thank you, Jesus, for Your Mercy and Grace!

19 | Maturity

The Scriptures describe the Three Steps of Christian Maturity (1 John 2:12–14).

Baby Christian

The Word teaches that we begin our Christian life as an infant in Christ. We are still full of the flesh and selfishness. In this stage, we learn that Jesus loves us and died for our sins. The Father reveals to us that our sins are forgiven, and that He doesn't remember them anymore (1 John 2:12). Amazing Grace! Like a newborn baby thirst for the milk of the Word, and we grow up quickly (1 Peter 2:2). We want to know our "Daddy," and we cry out for Him every day. We are protected by the Great Grace of our Father. We are young, and we think that God exists to meet our needs. We cry and fuss when we don't get our way. Our slogan is "It's all about me." Babies begin their life self-centered and dependent on their Heavenly Father for provi-

Blessed are those who wash their robes, that they may have the right to the tree of life and that they may enter the city by the gates. Revelation 22:14

sion. But there is a time to grow up. We can't stay in the crib for the rest of our life.

Young Men

These young men (or women) have now outgrown the baby stage, and they are becoming strong and overcoming the evil one (1 John 2:13). The Word of God is now abiding in them as they become doers of the Word (1 John 2:14). We leave the infant stage and begin to overcome the temptations of this world. The young men become great warriors doing battle for the Lord. These "spiritual teenagers" are disciplined by the Lord and are being changed into the image of Christ. The Father removes their proud selfish heart and places in them the heart of Jesus. They become strong in the Lord and stand upon His Word. These young men will not compromise their faith, but they stand up for the Truth in Love.

Fathers

The fathers started as babies and have grown up through the battles and trials of this life. They have been tested, and their faith is genuine. They are now strong in the Lord, and they begin to walk with God. These fathers know the Lord who is from the beginning (1 John 2:13). Like Moses, they have become a friend of God. They rest in His Presence, and they talk to God face-to-face. "Thus the Lord used to speak to Moses face to face, as a man speaks to his friend" (Exodus 33:11). God proclaims His friendship with Moses: "With him I speak mouth to mouth, clearly, and not in dark speech; and he beholds the form of the Lord" (Numbers 12.6–8). These fathers have found favor in God's sight, and He knows them by name (Exodus 33:17). They have a special intimacy with the Lord that few attain. As fathers, they begin to raise up and disciple many spiritual children. They become a godly example to all they meet. Like Enoch, they walk with God until He takes them to their Heavenly Home.

Spiritual Growth

The Word teaches that there are some Christians who refuse to grow up but choose to remain fleshly babies. The Scriptures warn that "though by this time they ought to be teachers, you need someone to teach you again the first principles of God's word" (Hebrews 5:11–14). Paul calls them carnal Christians who still live in the flesh and behave like the world (1 Corinthians 3:1–4). They should already be strong Christians, but they choose to stay immature so that they can indulge the desires of the flesh. They have little desire for the things of God but want to hear how Jesus can get them more money and possessions. It is time to grow up!

20 | The Power of the Tongue

The Lord takes His Word very seriously, but we are often careless with our tongues. I have often repented for my remarks spoken carelessly or in anger. The Father has instructed me to be careful with my words, but I still fall short. I used to justify my anger by saying that the other person "made me angry," but the Lord has taught me to take responsibility for my own tongue. I have no excuse. I can't blame others. The Scriptures warn that the power of life and death are in the tongue (Proverbs 18:21). We were created in the image of God who spoke the universe into existence by His Word. The Father stands behind every Word and every Promise that He makes. "Heaven and earth will pass away, but my words will not pass away" (Matthew 21:35). Unfortunately, we sometimes speak carelessly without thought of the consequences. The Bible warns that "on the day of judgment men will render account for every careless word they utter; for by your words you will be justified, and by your words you will be condemned" (Matthew 12:36–37). But where do those ugly words come from that are spoken in anger? The Bible tells us that they come from our hearts. "But what comes out of the mouth proceeds from the heart, and this defiles a man. For out of the heart come evil thoughts, murder, adultery, fornication, theft, false witness, slander" (Matthew 15:18–19).

Too often, we speak words of death—condemnation, judgment, doubt, fear, defeat, and failure. We have all used our mouths as a weapon to backbite, gossip, criticize, and judge. The Bible warns, "Let no evil talk come out of your mouths, but only such as is good for edifying, as fits the occasion, that it may impart grace to those who hear" (Ephesians 4:29). James informs us that our tongues are full of evil and poison that no man can tame. The Bible teaches that our words can become like the fires of hell. Sometimes, we act more like a fire-breathing dragon than a follower of Christ. The same passage describes how we sometimes use our mouths to bless God and then to curse those who are created in the image of God (James 3:3–12). Is our mouth "saved"? Is Jesus Lord over our tongue? Have we surrendered our mouths to God?

The Bible records an amazing story of how the evil report of eleven spies spread death to several million Israelites. The Father had led the Israelites out of Egypt and through the wilderness to bring them into the Promised Land. The Israelites came to the edge of Canaan and sent twelve spies into the area to see the land. Caleb brought back a report of faith encouraging the people to go into the land. Unfortunately, the other eleven spies brought back an evil report telling the Israelites that it was too dangerous to go into Canaan because of fortified cities and giants. The Israelites became afraid and refused to obey God. They started to complain and murmur, saying, "Would that we had died in the land of Egypt! Or would that we had died in this wilderness. Why does the Lord bring us into this land, to fall by the sword?" (Numbers 14:1–3. See chapters 13 and 14). Several million Israelites spoke their own death into existence. God heard their complaints and replied, "What you have said in my hearing I will do to you; your dead bodies shall fall in the wilderness" (Numbers 14:28–29). The Father granted their request, and all the Israelites over twenty died after wandering in the wilderness for forty years.

Christians can do the work of Satan the accuser when we use our mouths to accuse, judge, hate, condemn, put down, discourage, and bring fear and doubt. We must be careful to use our mouths to do God's work and not the work of the enemy. Satan's plan is to turn people against each other to bring division and destruction. Our mouths can become deadly weapons that hurt others and destroy relationships. The devil deceives marriage couples to attack each other with words of hate and accusation. Satan often tempts friends, family, and fellow Christians to accuse each other. Peter was even deceived by Satan to rebuke Jesus because he didn't understand the teaching of Jesus about the Cross. (Matthew 16:21–23). The Bible teaches us that God inhabits the praises of His people. Satan "inhabits" the words of hate, anger, judgment, and condemnation. I have also been convicted by the Holy Spirit for broken promises that I have made to Him and others. We sometimes make pledges to God in times of crisis, but then we soon forget our words when God delivers us. The Lord remembers every word and every promise that we make. Early in my ministry to the homeless, I used to make promises to help almost everyone in need. I had good intentions, but I didn't follow through with many of my commitments. The Holy Spirit told me to be careful with my words and not to make promises that I didn't intend to keep. Jesus came to this world filled with Grace and Truth (John 1:14). The enemy brings us condemnation by accusing us with the "truth"(accusation) without grace. We must learn to speak the Words of Jesus, which are full of love, encouragement, comfort, grace, faith, peace, goodness, kindness, and patience.

Isaiah saw a Glorious Vision of God's Holiness in the Temple, and he was immediately convicted of his sinful lips. The Lord sent an Angel to touch his mouth, "Behold, this has touched your lips; your guilt is taken away, and your sin forgiven" (Isaiah 6.1–7). I continue to pray, "Lord, touch my lips and take away the sinfulness of my mouth. Let my mouth be always filled with words of Love and Grace, never hate and condemnation and anger. O, Lord, sanctify my lips to proclaim words of Life, Faith, Freedom, and Victory. I want to encourage and build up all those who I meet. Touch my lips and purify my mouth. Let my words be Your Words."

21 | The Last Day Churches

The Father has called me to be a watchman and bring this warning to the Church (Ezekiel 3:16–21). I humbly bring this message to the Church in love before it is too late. There are many who are in danger of hearing Jesus say to them in the end, "I never knew you; depart from me, you evildoers" (Matthew 7:21–23). I cannot think of anything more frightening than having Jesus tell us to depart from Him for Eternity. Clearly, these people were deceived into thinking that they were right with God. They begin to say, "Lord, Lord, did we not prophesy in your name, and cast our demons in Your name, and do mighty works in your name" (Matthew 7:22). Jesus proclaims that they call Him Lord, but they are not obedient to Him. "Not everyone who says to me, 'Lord, Lord,' shall enter the kingdom of heaven, but he who does the will of my Father who is in heaven" (Matthew 7:21). Many have said a sinner's prayer with their lips, but their heart is still far from Him. They profess Jesus with their mouths but refuse to obey Him as Lord. The Word states that those who hear the Word but fail to do it are deceiving themselves (James 1:22–25).

I was born into American Dream Christianity, a mixture of the American culture and Christianity. In this false religion, Jesus exists to meet our needs. He is viewed as a "cosmic bellboy" or a "genie" who grants our wishes. The Truth is that Jesus is Lord and King, the Creator of all things! We exist to serve and worship Him! The Bible warns God's people to never adopt the pagan practices of the world around them (Colossians 2:8–9, 2 Kings 17:24–41). I was raised in

O LORD, our Lord, how majestic is Thy name in all the earth! Psalm 8.1

dead lukewarm religion, and the Bible was a dead book to me with stories of dead people. It all seemed like a strange fairy tale. One Sunday, I sat in a lifeless Church and opened up the songbook. I realized that the songs, prayers, and the sermon that we were using had been written by men over four hundred years ago. I asked in my heart, "What is God saying today? Is He still alive? Who is He, and what does He want me to do with my life?" The Gospel was still veiled to me because only through Christ is it taken away (2 Corinthians 3:12–16). I began to seek Him with all my heart, and by His Grace, the Father revealed Himself to me. I was not content with dead religion. I wanted a personal relationship with Jesus. The Lord disciplined me through the fire of a seven-year illness that burned away the lies of the American Dream Christianity. I had seen the Lord through the eyes of my materialistic culture, but in the valley of suffering and affliction, I began to truly see Him. Job wrote after his afflictions, "I had heard of thee by the hearing of the ear; but now my eye sees thee; therefore I despise myself, and repent in dust and ashes" (Job 42:5–6). I bow my knees in prayer, "O Lord, warn those who are lost in dead lukewarm religion before it is too late. Open their eyes to see the deception so that they can turn to You. Jesus, You opened my eyes when I was a sinner lost in the same deception. You delivered me from religion and brought me close to You. Take away the veil that covers their eyes through Christ. Let them come to You, repent, and find Salvation. Thank you, Jesus, for Your Grace and Mercy!"

The Laodicean Apostate Church

Jesus warns that in these last days, there will be a great falling away from Him and that many false Christs and false prophets will arise (Matthew 24:3–28). There will be an attempt by Satan to confuse and deceive those who live in these last days with false religion. The Bible warns that these "copies" of Christianity are only a shadow while the substance is Christ (Colossians 2:17. See 2:8–23). The Laodicean Lukewarm Church of today is in love with this world and not with Christ (Revelation 3:14–22). This Church teaches health, wealth, and prosperity and cries out, "I am rich, I have prospered, and I need nothing"(verse 3:17). They choose to worship the Golden Calf, which is the god of money and materialism instead of the True Living God (Exodus 32:1–20). Many desire to keep their life in this world and refuse to seek Heavenly things. Some ministers preach a "watered down, padded, pain free cross" where there is no suffering. This "cross" has Velcro instead of nails, padding on the wood, and a pillow for our heads. The Word of God has predicted this falling away: "For the time is coming when people will not endure sound teaching, but having itching ears they will accumulate for themselves teachers to suit their own likings, and will turn away from listening to the truth and wander into myths" (2 Timothy 4:3–4). Beloved, we must be careful not to accept this counterfeit Gospel. The Bible teaches that in these last days, there will be many who profess to be Christians but live worldly sinful lives. They have a form of godliness but deny the power of God to transform them into Christ's image. They attend Church but are not Christ-like. These make-believers are "lovers of self, lovers of money, proud, haters of good and lovers of pleasure rather than lovers of God" (2 Timothy 3.1–8). The Word of God tells us to avoid such people. "They profess to know God but deny them with their deeds (Titus 1:16). They attend Church but live like the world.

Paul warns the Bride of Christ, "But I am afraid that as the serpent deceived Eve by his cunning, your thoughts will be led astray from a sincere and pure devotion to Christ. For if someone comes and preaches another Jesus that the one we preached, or if you receive a different spirit than the one you received, or if you accept a different gospel from the one you accepted, you submit to it readily enough" (2 Corinthians 11:3–4). We are the Bride waiting for the Bridegroom to return, and we must be faithful to Him while we are still on this earth. We show our devotion to Christ by refusing to submit to those who teach another Jesus, another Gospel, and another Spirit. Paul wrote, "Even if we, or an angel from heaven, should preach to you a gospel contrary to that which we preached to you, let him be accursed" (Galatians 1:8).

The Lukewarm Church is filled with worldliness on the inside, while Jesus is on the outside knocking to get in. "Behold, I stand at the door and knock; if anyone hears my voice and opens the door, I will come in to him and eat with him, and he with me" (Revelation 3:20). This Church tries to live halfway between the world and Jesus. Jesus calls them hypocrites because they honor Him with their lips while their hearts are far from Him (Matthew 15:8–9). They have enough "religion" to think that they are saved, but they deceive themselves because they are only hearers of the Word, not doers (James 1:22–25). Their faith is dead because it doesn't produce fruit that is acceptable in God's sight (James 2:14–26). In the end, Jesus will say to the make-believers to depart from Him because He never knew them (Luke 13:23–27). Jesus states that He will spew (vomit) them out of His mouth (Revelation 3:16). We must have the heart of Jesus to seek the lost, who are in the Church as well and the lost who are in this world. I pray, "O Merciful Lord, open their eyes before it is too late. Send out Your Truth and Light to those in darkness. Deliver them from this deception so that they can turn to You."

The Philadelphia Remnant

Fortunately, there is a remnant in these last days who truly follow Christ. I have seen a Vision of this beautiful Church rising out of the rubble of the apostate Church. This Church remains faithful to the True Christ and the True Word of God. Jesus has set before these believers an open door into God's Presence. This remnant is called the Philadelphia Church in Revelation 3:7–13. The same door that is closed in the Laodicean Church is open to the Philadelphia Church. John went through this door in Revelation 4. "After this I looked, and lo, in heaven an open door! And the first voice which I had heard speaking to me like a trumpet, said, 'Come up hither, and I will show you what must take place after this.' At once, I was in the Spirit, and lo, a throne stood in heaven, with one seated on the throne!" (Revelation 4:1–2). Jesus called him up into God's Presence in the Spirit. Today, the Father has set this same door before the true followers of Christ. This remnant is given the privilege to come into His Presence at any time. They are called to come to Him and live before His Throne in Heavenly Places. When we walk with Him in the Spirit, our words, prayers, and actions have the authority of Jesus. We must learn to live, pray, and worship Him before the Throne of Grace.

The false gospel of health, wealth and prosperity is based on money, false prosperity and materialism. I was born into the materialism of this country, and as a self-centered child, I viewed God as a Santa Claus who existed to meet my needs. The Father has put me through years of discipline to burn away this cold, selfish heart and replace it with the heart of Jesus. As a youth, my goals were all for personal gain, but when I met Jesus, I counted everything as loss to gain Christ (Philippians 3:7–11). Gradually, the Lord burned away the selfish flesh, and He placed a servant's heart within me. The Father has always been faithful to provide for me as I have served Him.

God's Prosperity

The Father promises to Bless and provide for those who truly love Him and seek first His Kingdom. "But seek first his kingdom and his righteousness, and all these things shall be yours as well" (Matthew 6:33). There are many true followers of Christ who have laid down their idols of this world, and they are obedient to the Call of Jesus. They show their love for the Father by obeying His commandments. "If you love me, you will keep my commandments" (John 14:15). These believers worship God every day by offering themselves to Him as a living sacrifice. "I appeal to you therefore brethren, by the mercies of God, to present your bodies as a living sacrifice holy and acceptable to God, which is your spiritual worship" (Romans 12:1). They are content with God's provision for them on this earth. "But we brought nothing into the world, and we cannot take anything out of the world; but if we have food and clothing, with these we shall be content" (1 Timothy 6:6–10). These saints have surrendered their lives to Christ and left everything to follow Him (Matthew 16:24–25, Matthew 4:17–22, Mark 10:23–31).

Is Jesus Lord over our time, money, possessions, and our hearts? For years, I lived in fear of poverty and worked many hours a week to store up money. My faith was in the money instead of God. The Lord tested my heart and asked me to give my possessions away just as He did with the rich young ruler (Mark 10:17–22). By Grace of God, I left it all behind twenty-five years ago and followed Christ into inner city ministry. Everything now belongs to my Lord and Savior. It is now His money, His life, His time, and His possessions to do with as He pleases. Since the day that I let go of everything, the Father has blessed me and provided for my every need. Thank You, Jesus! He multiplied my finances like the loaves and the fishes (John 6.4–14. With His Blessing a hundred dollars now seems as if it is a thousand.

The Devil's "Prosperity"

As Christians, we are offered a counterfeit "prosperity" that comes from the devil. The Bible makes it clear that whenever we love the things of this world, we are bowing down and serving the enemy. Jesus was tempted with the glory of this world in the wilderness, "And the devil took Him up and showed him all the kingdoms of this world in a moment of time, and said to him, 'To you I will give all this authority and their glory; for it has been delivered to me and I give it to whom I will. If you, then, will worship me, it shall all be yours.' And Jesus answered him, 'It is written, "You shall worship the Lord your God, and him only shall you serve"' (Luke 4:8). The enemy makes the same offer to God's people, if they will serve and worship him. I will bow down to the Most High God, and I refuse to serve any other god. The Father originally gave this earth to Adam and his descendants, but this authority was lost through sin. The devil has stolen man's dominion over this earth and now offers it back to us in exchange for our Eternal souls. The Word warns, "For what will it profit a man, if he gains the whole world and forfeits his life?"

(Matthew 16:6). "We know that we are of God, and the whole world is in the power of the evil one" (1 John 5:19). Through Christ, we can be restored to our rightful place as caretakers of God's creation. When we seek Jesus with all our hearts, He gives us the authority to Reign with Him on this earth, and He promises to provide for all our needs.

The Bible teaches that the Lord will withhold His blessing upon those who put the things of this world before Him. Our money is put into a bag with holes in it and our finances and possessions shrink into nothing (Haggai 1:2–11). We cannot serve God and money at the same time. If you are devoted to money, then you will despise God, and if you love God, you will despise money (Matthew 6:24). The Word states that if we love this world, we do not love God because all that is in the world is not of God (1 John 2:15–17).

I have found that it is easy to be drawn into materialism and idolatry because we are surrounded by a world of selfishness and greed. I pray, "Lord, please keep my heart pure and unstained by this world. Let my desire be only for You. I lay down my life in this world in hope of a new life in Your Heavenly Kingdom. I will worship only You! I will not bow down to any other altar or serve any other god. You alone are worthy to be praised. I will not compromise or become distracted by this world. I will finish the race, and I will keep the faith. I choose to do Thy Will O God. I choose to love only You."

22 | Doers of the Word

The Scriptures warn that many hear the Word, but they never become doers of the Word. The Scriptures teach that the Word didn't benefit them because "it didn't meet with faith in the hearers" (Hebrews 4:2). These hearers deceive themselves, and their faith is dead (James 1:22–25, 2:14–26). The Bible teaches that true faith produces fruit. Our actions on the outside show what we believe on the inside. Some modern Churches have become large "hearer theaters" for entertaining spectators instead of the True Biblical model of the Body of Christ. Some Churches are filled with people who sit back and watch a show for an hour and then return to their lives in this world. The Church that puts on the best show becomes the most popular. Many of these hearers spend their one hour of "God time" on Sunday and then spend the rest of the week living for themselves. These hearers are still in control of their lives and refuse to surrender to Christ. Many have become too busy with the world to study His Word, pray, and worship the Lord outside of Church. These seeker-friendly Churches are the product of the world around them. We live in a society that seeks intellectual knowledge and entertainment. Many people have become spectators that sit in front of TVs, computers, phones, movies, and video game screens. The Word of God reveals that in these last days, "Many shall run to and fro, and knowledge shall increase" (Daniel 12:4). Many seek knowledge through the Internet but few truly seek God. The Word states that they will "listen to anybody and can never arrive at a knowledge of the truth (2 Timothy 3:7). The Bible warns that knowledge puffs up, but love builds up (1 Corinthians 8:1). We can study the Bible, attend Church, and know about God, but do we truly have a relationship with Him? Do we walk with Him during the week or only seek Him for an hour on Sunday?

The Word of God describes the True model for the Church. Jesus is the Head of the Body, and He has given gifts and ministries to each one according to His Will. The Lord has called each to minister to others members of the Body of Christ and to fulfill His Great Commission to reach the lost in this world (1 Corinthians 12:12–31, Romans 12:4–8, Ephesians 4:11–13). There is no ministry of pew sitting in the True Church. No one is called to be a spectator. Every part of the Body is important and needed by the other members. The Body grows up into Christ and is joined and knit together when each member is working properly (Ephesians 4:15–16). The Holy Spirit should be free to move and minister in the Church. A hearer is a spectator, while the doer steps out by faith and is Anointed by God to do the work of the ministry. True followers of Christ walk with him every day—24-7—and not just on Sunday.

There is a story that illustrates the difference between a hearer and a doer. In this example, a man (Jesus) is attempting to walk across a wire that is stretched across Niagara Falls. There are many spectators watching nearby. Jesus asks them whether they believe that He can walk across the wire to the other side and back. The crowd shouts, "Yes." He walks across and returns to them to ask them if they believe that He can do this with a wheelbarrow. They again answer, "Yes." He successfully walks across and returns to the crowd and asks them whether they think that He can walk across with the wheelbarrow filled with two hundred pounds. They answer "Yes" again. Jesus then tells them to get in. There was only one man who had true faith in Jesus to get into the wheelbarrow. The spectators were the hearers who cheered from afar. The doer was the man who got into the wheelbarrow. Which one are we? Do we sit in the pews and cheer for Jesus, or do we put our lives into His Hands and trust Him with everything?

23 | Unconditional Love

God is Love. (1 John 4:8). He loves everyone unconditionally in a world that is filled with hate. He loves us regardless of how we behave or what we do. He loves us the same when we fail as when we succeed. He loves us on our good days and on our bad days. He loves us regardless of money, appearance, or social standing. He loves us when we win and when we lose. He loves us when we love Him and when we don't. He loves us when we won't even acknowledge His existence. This is the Father's Amazing Love that sent Jesus to die on the Cross while we were yet sinners (1 John 4:9).

We live in the last days when wickedness is multiplied and most men's love has grown cold (Matthew 24:12). Wickedness and sin has removed most men's love from this earth. Man's "love" is selfish, con-

In Pursuit of God | Unconditional Love

You will seek Me and find Me; when you seek me with all your heart.
Jer. 29.13

ditional, full of lust and perversion. Human love says, " I will love you as long as it meets my needs or as long as I choose to." This human love will always fail and has caused many marriages to end in divorce. The original Greek language uses the word Agape to describe God's unconditional love. In our culture, the word love has lost its meaning. We say I "love" hot dogs or I "love" this movie. We also use the word "love" to describe lustful sexual immorality. We made "love." The Word of God has a completely different definition of love: "love is patient and kind; love is not jealous or boastful; it is not arrogant or rude. Love does not insist on its own way; it is not irritable or resentful; it does not rejoice at wrong, but rejoices in the right. Love bears all things, believes all things, hopes all things, endures all things" (1 Corinthians 13:4–7). The Father values true love above all else (1 Corinthians 13:13), and yet it is clear from the Scriptures that true love is rare in this world.

The Father has called His Church to love others unconditionally so that the world may see the Love of Christ and turn to Him. The Holy Spirit fills our hearts with God's Agape Love so that we can love our enemies, do good to those who hate us, bless those who curse us, pray for those who abuse us, and give to those who beg from us (Luke 6:27–38, Romans 5:5). His love changes our hearts so that we begin to forgive and not condemn, to give and not take. We become servants to others and put their needs before our own. We will no longer judge but show mercy to everyone. Christ's Love in us will change the world!

This unconditional love needs to begin at home in our marriages and families (Ephesians 5:21–33). We must seek to serve and not to be served, to love and not be loved, to give and not to receive. We look to forgive and not be forgiven, to respect and not to be respected. We put the needs of others before our own. "As you wish that men would do to you, do so to them" (Luke 6:31). The Father commands us to forgive immediately when we are wronged as Jesus did when He was on the Cross. We seek not to argue with our spouses because love does no harm to others (Romans 13:10). Instead, God has called us to walk in love, give and serve others, regardless of how we are treated in return. The Father has called us to love our spouses unconditionally by serving, giving, putting their needs first, yielding, respecting, and forgiving them unconditionally. We fall short every day, but we seek for God's Spirit to pour His Love onto us to transform marriages, households, and all relationships.

The Love of Jesus on the Cross overcame the power of sin, hate, and death. When we walk with God, we walk in love, and we overcome all evil. "Do not be overcome by evil, but overcome evil with good" (Romans 12:21. See Romans 12:14–21). The enemy gains a foothold in our lives when we allow bitterness and anger into our hearts. We walk in His Victory when we walk in His Love. I pray, "O Lord, give me the Grace to always love, forgive, show mercy, bless, serve, and give to others. Lord, never let bitterness, anger, and unforgiveness take root in my life and overcome me. Let Your Love flow out of my heart like Living Waters to those in need."

24 | The Resurrection

In 1996 the Lord allowed me to experience the power of His resurrection when I was lifted up by the Holy Spirit in an amazing way and I looked down at my body standing on the ground fifty feet below. I believe this was a vision of our resurrection when Jesus returns. God's amazing Plan for the Church is to be raised up with Christ. "Lo! I tell you a mystery. We shall not all sleep, but we shall all be changed, in a moment, in the twinkling of an eye, at the last trumpet. For the trumpet will sound, and the dead will be raised imperishable, and we shall be changed" (1 Corinthians 15:51–52). The words in the Bible that are translated, changed, transformed, and transfigured are from the same root word in the Greek from which we get the English word metamorphosis. This expression is often used to describe the amazing transformation from a caterpillar to a butterfly.

Christ will transform us in a similar way. We begin with the fallen sinful nature of Adam (caterpillar) and are then changed into the image of Christ (butterfly). Paul writes, "Just as we have borne the image of the man of dust, we shall also bear the image of the man of heaven" (1 Corinthians. 15:49). Our weak, perishable physical body will be raised to an imperishable Glorious spiritual body (1 Corinthians 15:42–50). Jesus will change our lowly body to be like Christ's Glorious Body. (Philippians 3.21). Soon, God will dwell with His people Forever and make all things new. He will wipe away all tears, death, mourning, crying and pain (Revelation 21:3–5. The Word teaches that the same Resurrection Power that raised Jesus from the grave is in us who believe (Ephesians 1:16–23).

Jesus showed us a Vision of our future Resurrection when He was transfigured on the mountain from His human form to His Glorious Heavenly Body (Luke 9:28–36). The Word makes it clear that this transformation begins in us when we are Born Again, continues for the remainder of our lives, and is completed at Christ's Return. "And we all, with unveiled face, are being changed into his likeness from one degree of glory to another; for this comes from the Lord who is the Spirit" (2 Corinthians 3:18). The Spirit of God is gradually transforming all believers on this earth into the image of Christ. The caterpillar goes into the cocoon and emerges through a small hole with wings and flies away. The caterpillar must struggle to go through this hole so that the blood is pushed into its wings so it is able to fly. If someone cuts open the cocoon to let out the butterfly, it will have wings but never fly. Some Christians have the potential to fly but choose instead to walk in the flesh. We also must struggle in this life to let go of the sin nature and become like Christ. The Word warns us not to be conformed to this world but to be transformed by the renewal of our minds (Romans 12.2). We will experience the Resurrection Power of Christ only after we are united with Christ on the Cross. "For if we have been united with him in a death like his, we shall certainly be united with him in a resurrection like his" (Romans 6:5). Paul writes that he chose to, "share in his sufferings, becoming like him in his death, that if possible, I may attain the resurrection from the dead" (Philippians 3:10–11). If we are willing to lay down our lives in this world, then we will begin to "fly" with Christ in the Resurrection. Jesus is alive, and the grave is empty! Thank you, Lord, for the amazing miracle of the Resurrection!

The Scriptures are clear that there is life after death for all men. Those who have "done good, to the resurrection of life, and those who have done evil, to the resurrection of judgment" (John 5:29). Luke gives a look behind the veil and reveals the final destination of believers and unbelievers. In this story, there is a rich man who enjoyed everything he wanted in this life but had no faith in the Lord. He lost his soul, perished, and woke up in Hades where he was in torment. In the same story, there was a homeless man named Lazarus who loved God but suffered without mercy on the street outside his gate. Lazarus also died but was carried with Angels to Paradise where he was rewarded for his faith (Luke 16:19–31). The Book of Revelation reveals the future of both men. The rich man will stand before the Great White Throne and be judged for all that he has done and then spend Eternity separated from God in the lake of fire (Revelation 20:11–15). In contrast, Jesus will return for Lazarus, and he will be placed in the New Jerusalem where he will spend Eternity in God's Glorious Presence. (Revelation 21 and 22).

There is no need for any to perish when we can turn to Christ at any time and be forgiven for our sins. The choice is ours: Eternity in the Glorious Presence of God or separated from Him Forever. I pray, "O Lord, let me spend Eternity with You. Come back for me and take me to Your Glorious New Land. In Your Grace and Mercy, raise me up into Your Presence Forever. Lord, thank you for Your Resurrection. Without Your Grace, I would perish."

Truly, God is Good!

25 |
The Prayers of Repentance

Forty-four years ago, the Lord appeared to me in Glory with angels all around me. When I experienced God's Holiness and Righteousness, I realized that I was full of sin. As Isaiah wrote after seeing the Lord, "Woe is me! For I am lost; for I am a man of unclean lips, and I dwell in the midst of a people of unclean lips; for my eyes have seen the King, the LORD of hosts!" (Isaiah 6:5). The Holy Spirit brought light into the darkness of my soul, and I was convicted of my pride and sinfulness. During this time, I wrote many prayers to God, crying out for mercy to be set free from the power of sin through the blood of Christ. When the Lord called me, He revealed to me that He had chosen me. For many years I have struggled with feelings of unworthiness. The Lord put a passion in my heart to know Him, and I cried out to God to remove anything in me that was not of Him. I can look back now and realize that God has Faithfully answered all my prayers.

"O Most High God, one thing I desire of You that I may dwell in Your Presence all the days of my life and behold Your Face. I desire to stand face-to-face with the Most High God, the God of Eternity who lives in the High and Holy place. I will kneel before You in humbleness and shame and cry out for Mercy. I fall down upon my face and plead for Your Mercy to save my very life; but You have heard my cry and said, 'Come, follow Me.' You have saved me. You reached down and plucked my soul from death that I may serve You throughout Eternity. Lord, I run after You as a child runs after his father. There are times when I stumble and fall. In my enthusiasm, I sometimes stray away from You. I come back to You downcast and shameful. But I look into Your eyes and see love, not hate; acceptance, and not rejection. My eyes fill with tears of joy because I am the most fortunate son in all the world to have a Father like You. "Lord, I come to You as a little child. I lay the burdens of my life at Your feet. All that I have struggled for seems to vanish in the air. I am left with emptiness and despair. I turn back to look at the lifeless body I left lying on the ground. But all thoughts disappear as I turn to face You. I look in Your eyes and thoughts of myself vanish in Your embrace. Lord, why me? Why did you choose me to be Your son? Who am I that You would want to dwell in Me? Why use me for Your Holy Eternal Purpose? It is because of Your Mercy that You chose one who was as lost as me. Your tender Arms of love reached down to pick up my sad and lonely soul. You chose to dwell in this hopeless failure of a man. Just one touch from You and the spark of Your Life burst

forth enveloping the old and creating the new. A new creation of life sprang forth from death. Resurrection! Hope!

I have served myself, other gods and many idols. With my pride, I have bowed down to many altars less than the Altar of the Most High God. The pride of my flesh has served fear. **But it is time to serve the Most High God. I will bow down before His Altar and His Altar only, for He alone is worthy to be served.** Consider Your servant, O Lord. Hear my cry, O God; for my strength is spent and my soul has run dry. But Thou, O Lord, art my strength and my salvation. I will hope only in Thee. With all my toil and work, I can do nothing to save myself. I kneel before You and cry for help. My soul is empty, and my strength is spent. Renew my spirit. Give me Your Strength to serve You all the days of my life. All my times are in Your hands. Use Your servant to bring glory to Your Name. I will praise Thee all the days of my life for Thou are faithful to Thy servant. Lord, I am so weak. I am but a frail, hollow, lifeless leaf at the mercy of the wind to blow me to some unknown place. I cry for help, but the words fall hopelessly to the ground in silence. People pass by me, some smile but all go on their way. Who would stop for me? The world outside looks at me with cold, mocking eyes. I turned inside for warmth, but I found that cold also. I tried to run and hide, but there was nowhere to go, no one to embrace. Am I so different? What is wrong with me? Someone made a mistake when they created me. Someone did create me. Where is He? I turn my eyes upward, and Your tender Arms embrace me. His touch of Love fills all the emptiness inside me. Let Your cleansing Presence envelope me that I may behold the peaceful awe of Your Beauty. As I approach You, everything fades away in the reality of the Presence of the Most High God. Your glorious fire consumes all else. By Your Grace, I can stand in the midst of the Almighty God to behold the terror of Your Majesty. As I bathe in the sea of Your Presence, my filthiness is enveloped in Your embrace and is consumed. Lord, save me from this pride. I try so hard to serve You, but all my efforts fail. Why is all this evil in me? Where does it come from? Free me, Lord, heal me and wash me clean. I thank you for the afflictions that You sent to me to crush and destroy my pride. Consume me with Your Holy fire. There is no good thing within me, for only You are Good. But now I am good because You dwell within me. Lord, I repent of my pride; take it from me. I cry out for mercy. I cast myself before Your Throne and beg for the Blood of the Lamb to cleanse me. I praise the Lamb because He made a way to the Father through His Blood. Forgive me, cleanse me with Your Blood, wash me completely clean that I may be Your perfect Bride without spot or blemish. I long to be transparent, with Your Presence and Love radiating out of me. I desire to be completely pure with no areas of darkness so I can glorify Your name. I don't know what to say before You. All words seem empty and powerless. You know my heart, O Lord. My heart is turned toward You, and it desires You. Lord, see this feeble attempt as I reach out with my weakened arms toward You and cry Your for Mercy. I am deceitful and wicked. My pride wells up within me again just as I think I am free of it. I hate my sinfulness because it lifts itself up against You. It comes from the depths of a fallen heart. Against You only have I sinned. Before You only do I repent. The Lord is the Living Almighty God. The roar of His Power is heard throughout the universe. Who can stand against the Most High God? Have mercy upon me, O God. My years are spent in sorrow. My burden is great, and my strength has failed within me.

I am made from the dust of the earth. Hear from Heaven, O Mighty One. Touch me with healing. Take away my shame. Let Your healing come with wings to lift me toward You. Swing wide the Gate and let the King of Glory come in. Break the chains, loosen the shackles, and free me from bondage. Let me soar into the heavens that I may serve You with all my whole being. Have Mercy upon me, O Lord, deliver me from my sorrow. Only You can heal me. Only You can save me. Praise the Lord for He considers the afflictions of His people.

I stand in awe of my sinfulness and how blind I have been to see any good in me. How blind I have been of You. I have run from Your Light because it exposed my darkness. I have lived a lie and constructed an illusion as I shielded myself from Your Truth. In my shame, I have made a false idol of myself. I have turned things and people into idols, but they can't save me. I come now in shame to You: the only True Living God. In Your Mercy, let me live. Let Your true Life in me rise above the dark rubble of my life. Your Life in me is my only hope. As I face the truth about myself, I can see Your Truth in me. Lord, let my life express Your Will. Let my words and actions manifest only You. Cast all else far away from me. Deliver me from the enemies that seek to possess, control, and manipulate me. Crush all that pulls me away from Your Will. Let your Light shine upon the darkness and confusion. Let Your Word be a lamp unto my feet that I might walk only in Your Path. Build Your fortress around me, repair the walls, restore the gates that no enemies can get in. Lord, send me to the world that is dying. They cry for help, yet they don't see. They are suffocating in their hopelessness, pain and despair. The stench of death is everywhere. People with cold, hard, tightly drawn faces exchange only short glances as they stumble in the dark groping for help. They become more frantic and determined as every ounce of life is choked out of them. Lord, let Your Living Word come as a sharp two-edged sword to cut away the falsehoods and the games. We have built false structures made by our own hands. Our religiousness has replaced Your Presence. We have become sad empty shells that have long since lost Your Life. We continue building higher and higher, more and more. Sometimes, we hesitate to wonder why You are not there anymore, but we press on with our imitations of You. Building, building; hurry, hurry; but where, where? A voice comes forth in the midst of the scurry and confusion. It is so calm and peaceful that no one seems to listen. Only a few turn to listen. 'Stop what you are doing and come to Me. Leave it all behind and follow Me. I will become all things to you. Your building must fall and burn. For behold, I am building a House that cannot be shaken. For I alone am the builder. All things must be subjected to me so that I may be everything to everyone for I alone am the source; in Me is Life. I alone am your portion. What else do you need? Am I not enough? For I am the Lord your God. Besides Me, there is no other. Therefore, seek only Me; for I am your God.'

Lord, make me a transparent Bride without spot or wrinkle—a true reflection of Christ without any imperfections or areas of darkness—so that I may show Your Glory upon this earth and spread the glorious knowledge of Your Holiness. When I walk, let it be You walking. When I speak, let it be You speaking. When I live, let it be You living. I want to be a visible manifestation of Your precious Love, a standard of Your Righteousness, and an expression of Your Holiness. I ask to be like Christ so that people may see and hear You in me. Lord, entrust Your work with me for You are faithful to complete it. Fill this vessel with Your Power to fulfill Your Will upon this earth. My efforts will fail, but You will accomplish Your Will through me, and it will succeed. I stand before You naked. I strip away all pride, strength, ambition, and self-assurance. I lay down my goodness and all my strivings. They are lying on the ground in one hopeless heap as filthy rags. I cry out for You to clothe me for I am naked. Cover me in my shame. Behold from Heaven came a white robe of Righteousness. The living clothes of Jesus Christ enveloped me and covered my nakedness. A new Life embraced me. I fell to my knees and cried, 'Holy, Holy is our God, the Source of all Life. He alone is Righteous. Worship the Most High God. Who is worthy to stand in His Presence but he who has been cleansed by the Lamb? The Lamb alone is worthy.' Lord, I embrace Your creation because it expresses You—Your Joy, Your Beauty, and Your Love. What a privilege to be blessed with such a reflection of your nature. It is so complex and yet so beautifully simple. There is so much to see and so much to know. I become frantic to absorb it all in, but I don't have time. I slow down and rest in Your Peace. God will always be there with me. I am blessed to know the Author of all things and the Father of the universe. I am not worthy, and yet by Grace, I am. For it has pleased God to reveal Himself to me in the form of His Son. I bask as the immeasurable riches of Your Presence envelope me. The highest purpose for my life is to know the Most High God. I enter Your Presence and leave all else behind. All else is consumed in the creative Power of Your Holiness. Who can stand in the Presence of the Most High God? I can only fall down and worship and cry out for Mercy. Praise God for He has heard my prayers that I might know Him. He called me His son even though I am a fallen sinful creature. By His Mercy, I will dwell Forever in the infinite expanse of His Presence."

Truly, God is Good!

26 | The Path Set Before Me

I am now near the end of my journey and I can look back forty-six years ago at the passion that the Lord put in my heart to know Him. The journey was more difficult than I realized- but also more glorious. In my early years as a follower of Christ, Jesus called me to leave behind the path that led to destruction and follow Him on the Path of Life. "Enter by the narrow gate; for the gate is wide and the way is easy, that leads to destruction, and those who enter by it are many. For the gate is narrow and the way is hard, that leads to life and those who find it are few" (Matthew 7:13–14). Thankfully, by the Grace of God, I chose to follow Jesus at a young age. God has been faithful to give me the strength to run the race set before me for over forty years (1 Corinthians 9:24–27). As a youth, Jesus gave me these words to describe the struggle that I had making the choice to follow Christ. As I read this now, I realize that I was young in my faith and fearful of the cost of following Christ.

"I stand at the place of decision asking which road should I follow and which way should I go? So many choices- I struggle to keep up with the fast pace of this life. There is too much to see, too much to know but where will it end? But somehow through the clamor and confusion I see an ancient path covered with ivy, lined with oaks; with a stream flowing beside it. Not much traffic, a lonely road; who would go down it? There is something compelling about this one; something draws me to it. There is a beckoning deep within my soul. An old voice and yet something wonderfully new. I feel inadequate- I could never do it, it is too hard. I would rather stay with what is familiar? Somehow, I know that to choose this road would cost everything- the path is old and narrow, it is steep- over many mountains and down many valleys. Yet I realize that it is the only way and the only answer. But then I look down at myself and I begin to doubt whether I am able to walk the path after years on the wide and flat path. I stand here alone: the others have gone and I fall to my knees and then to my face and my tears mix with the dust of the earth. I am without hope- everything is gone and the past has faded away. It all seems so meaningless as I face this decision. But at this point of lowest despair, a still small voice speaks to my heart that there is hope, there is life. The voice tells me to come, but I feel so hopeless and I think that it is a mistake for Him to choose me. The voice of the Lord tells me to come and a spark of hope touches me, I slowly look up towards the road and I see a Man standing in the distance! Someone has made it! Jesus has walked down the path! He is alone. no one has walked it with Him. His eyes are Love. He tells me that

He has walked this road for me and He promises to walk with me. I hesitate for a moment because I think the path is too difficult. Again, He calls me to come and I take the first step as His Love fills me. I am known. I have known Him always; yet I have never known Him. All is new; the joy of simplicity and peace. It is all from Him. The road continues and I continue to stop to eat the fruit that grows along the path for nourishment and strength. The road gets harder but He is there to prepare the way. He goes before me and leads me through the valleys and over the mountains. My concern is Him and no longer the path He takes. It is no longer me but Him."

27 | The Final Journey

I have entered the final season of my life, and God has been faithful through it all. "Even to your old age, I am he, and to gray hairs I will carry you. I made, and I will bear; I will carry and save" (Isaiah 46:4). By His Grace, I found Him in my youth when my body and mind were strong. God has been with me through all the seasons of my life. I thank Him for all things, even for the valleys when He called me to suffer. This, too, was part of His Plan. I long to hear the words of the Master say to me, "Well done, good and faithful servant; you have been faithful over a little, I will set you over much; enter into the joy of your master" (Matthew 25:21). O how I long to please the Father with my life! It is only by His Grace that my life can glorify the Father. I am content with the time that I have spent with Him on this earth. It has been an honor to know Him and walk with Him like Enoch. I would seek no other path than the one He set before me. I am so grateful that He chose me. My heart yearns to see Him face-to-face. In my youth, I had asked Him many questions, and He told me that many things must now remain a mystery so that I could live by faith. He has promised me that one day, we will meet on a mountain top in Heaven, and He will reveal all these things to me. I long for that day! I am now content with what He has shown me, but I continue to seek for more of Him.

God has called me to write this account of His Goodness toward me in this life and to describe the Visions of the age that is to come. Soon, the seventh trumpet will sound, and there will be a shout in Heaven, "The kingdom of the world has become the kingdom of our Lord and of his Christ and he shall reign for ever and ever" (Revelation 11:15). These wonderful experiences and these Visions were gifts from God that He has asked me to share with His Church. They were

Make me to know Thy ways, O LORD; teach me Thy Paths. Psalm 25:4

a look into the Glory that is to be fully revealed to us in Heaven. As His Church, we set our Hope on this Glorious Inheritance that is prepared for us in Christ. All that we suffered on this earth was not in vain, and a reward is waiting for us in Heaven.

My life took an unexpected turn over four years ago when I was diagnosed with stage four Waldenstrom's Non-Hodgkin's Lymphoma. I continue to thank God and praise Him every day in the midst of cancer and pain. The cancer has caused eleven compression fractures of my vertebrae, but I continue to walk by faith and I see His Glory every day. There is still a passion that burns in my heart to know Him. My plan was to continue to work with the homeless and minister in the jails, but my life abruptly changed when I suffered a compression fracture two years ago in my L5 vertebrae. I underwent back surgery and the surgeon expected me to return to work in ten days. Instead, my back condition continued to deteriorate and I was unable to move and I sat in a chair for five months in extreme pain. The cancer had spread to ninety percent of my bone marrow in my back and it began to cause ten more fractures of my vertebrae. The pain caused me to cry out to Jesus and draw even closer to Him. I need Jesus every day. He raised me up by His resurrection power and I began to walk with my walker every morning. In 2021, Jesus gave me a vision of healing when I was walking last year. I saw a Scripture come down out of heaven into me, "He sent forth his word and healed them" (Psalms 107:20). This illness has been another step in my journey to know Christ. Every day is a miracle as He raises me up to overcome cancer. Truly, He has been faithful to me in the midst of great suffering. This illness has been a test of faith and I am no longer able to work or minister in the jails. The Lord has opened up a door for me to minister on Facebook through prayer, support and Bible Study videos. When I was diagnosed with stage four cancer, I heard a voice that said "you have served God for twenty-five years, it is time to go home". At first it sounded good to be free from the pain and come home to Jesus, but then I later realized that this was the voice of the enemy telling me to give up. I decided to live by this cancer motto: give it to God, live one day at a time and try to help as many people as I can every day. I will be here as long as the Lord wants me to serve Him and then the angels will take me home to the Presence of God where I will be Forever. I can only imagine the indescribable Joy that will be in my heart when He comes for me. He will call my name, and I will be raised with Christ. What I had believed in from afar on this earth will then become my Eternal reality. I will shout, "I was not deceived, all that God told me is true! Nothing will ever separate me from Him again. He has wiped away all tears, sorrow, pain and death. Everything is made new as we are enveloped in the Joy of His Presence. The Father has desired to dwell in us Forever and the Church will shine as stars throughout Eternity. There is still a passion that burns in my heart to know Him. and He is still with me after all these years. Thank You, Jesus! I long to put off this body of death and to be clothed with the Righteousness of Christ (Philippians 3:20–22). We will shout, "Death is swallowed up in victory. O death, where is thy victory? O death, where is thy sting?" Thanks be to the Lord who always gives us Victory through Christ (1 Corinthians 15:54–57).I long to be able to proclaim, like Paul, at the end of my life that I have finished the race and kept the faith. "I have fought the good fight, I have finished the race, I have kept the faith. Henceforth there is laid up for me the crown of righteousness, which the

Lord, the righteous judge, will award to me on that Day, and not only to me but to all who have loved his appearing" (2 Timothy 4:7–8).

God will raise us up with Christ and make all things new. We will be given a new, glorious body that is like Christ's Body. He will purify our hearts and minds, and there will no longer be any sin in us or around us. God will remove even the possibility of sin so we will no longer be afraid. All Glory goes to the Lamb that was slain. I have seen Him in this life through a glass that is darkened by sin and imperfection, but I will spend Eternity face-to-face with Him (1 Corinthians 13:12). God will fulfill all His promises to me (Psalm 138:8). What a Truly Amazing Loving God that we serve! O how I long to be with Him Forever!

The Lord will fulfill his promise to me three years ago, "You will rise, Peter, you will rise above them all'. This year Jesus spoke to me: "You will be the one who rises, Peter". The Father has promised that He will raise me up above all my enemies and all the suffering of this life to spend eternity with Him. "As for me, I shall behold thy face in righteousness; when I awake, I shall be satisfied with beholding thy form" (Psalm 17:15). In this Hope, I live, that when I awake, I will be satisfied because I will be righteous in Christ, and I will see His Face! Thank you, Jesus!

Truly, God is Good!

Also by Peter Schuler

Warrior for Christ: Overcoming Cancer By Faith

Warrior for Christ: Overcoming Cancer by Faith is the inspirational story of how Peter Schuler is walking by faith in God to overcome incurable Stage 4 cancer that has caused eleven compression fractures of his vertebrae. Every day, Jesus does a miracle and lifts Peter up to walk with severe back pain. This book describes how Jesus has healed Peter of a near-terminal illness, a crippling injury, and childhood trauma. Peter shares how Jesus called him twenty-five years ago to minister to the homeless and those in jails and nursing homes.

www.ingramcontent.com/pod-product-compliance
Lightning Source LLC
Chambersburg PA
CBHW061201070526
44579CB00009B/85